Getting
the Grant

How Educators Can Write
Winning Proposals and
Manage Successful Projects

REBECCA GAJDA and RICHARD TULIKANGAS

Association for Supervision and Curriculum Development
Alexandria, Virginia USA

Association for Supervision and Curriculum Development
1703 N. Beauregard St. • Alexandria, VA 22311-1714 USA
Phone: 800-933-2723 or 703-578-9600 • Fax: 703-575-5400
Web site: www.ascd.org • E-mail: member@ascd.org
Author guidelines: www.ascd.org/write

Gene R. Carter, Executive Director; Nancy Modrak, Director of Publishing; Julie Houtz, Director of Book Editing & Production; Deborah Siegel, Project Manager; Media Plus Design, Graphic Designer; Keith Demmons, Typesetter; Vivian Coss, Production Specialist

All Web links in this book are correct as of the publication date below but may have become inactive or otherwise modified since that time. If you notice a deactivated or changed link, please e-mail books@ascd.org with the words "Link Update" in the subject line. In your message, please specify the Web link, the book title, and the page number on which the link appears.

ASCD Member Book, No. FY05-09 (August 2005, P). ASCD Member Books mail to Premium (P), Comprehensive (C), and Regular (R) members on this schedule: Jan., PC; Feb., P; Apr., PCR; May, P; July, PC; Aug., P; Sept., PCR; Nov., PC; Dec., P.

Paperback ISBN: 1-4166-0172-4 • ASCD product #104001 • e-books retail PDF ISBN: 1-4166-0307-7 • netLibrary ISBN 1-4166-0305-0 • ebrary ISBN 1-4166-0306-9

Quantity discounts for the paperback book: 10–49 copies, 10%; 50+ copies, 15%; for 500 or more copies, call 800-933-2723, ext. 5634, or 703-575-5634.

Library of Congress Cataloging-in-Publication Data

Gajda, Rebecca.
  Getting the grant : how educators can write winning proposals and manage successful projects / Rebecca Gajda and Richard Tulikangas.
      p. cm.
  Includes bibliographical references and index.
  ISBN 1-4166-0172-4 (alk. paper)
  1. Educational fund raising--United States--Handbooks, manuals, etc. 2. Proposal writing for grants--United States--Handbooks, manuals, etc. 3. Proposal writing in education--United States--Handbooks, manuals, etc. I. Tulikangas, Richard. II. Title.

      LC243.A1.G35 2005
      379.1'3--dc22
                                          2005010279

12 11 10 09 08 07 06 05   12 11 10 9 8 7 6 5 4 3 2 1

Getting the Grant

How Educators Can Write Winning Proposals and Manage Successful Projects

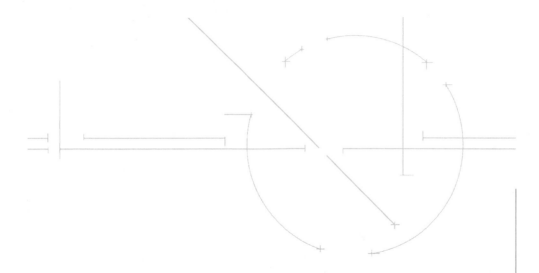

Introduction

You can do this! That's our motto for this book, which is designed to be an informative and engaging resource that explains not only how to get a grant, but also, of equal importance, what to expect and do after you "get the call." We offer a unique insider's perspective on the subject because of our extensive experience with grant writing, grant reviewing, grant evaluation, and grant sustainability. We know from our own experience that getting project grants and sustaining those projects is less daunting than most people think.

The book is for education and social service practitioners at all levels of experience with grant writing and project sustainability. The intended audience includes principals, teachers, administrators, curriculum directors, directors of nonprofits, evaluators, grant coordinators, case managers, special educators, and college faculty members who want to find and secure project funding and to collaboratively sustain their efforts long into the future. The book incorporates useful tools such as worksheets, matrixes, frameworks, checklists, and rubrics that you can use and adapt for your own purposes.

We do not want to mislead you: *Effective grant writing and project sustainability take a considerable amount of time and energy, but they require common sense and attention to detail—not rocket science.*

What Compels Us to Write This Book?

As authors, we bring our own perspectives, experiences, and values to the book. Everything we suggest, all the information we provide, and every key point we make is a reflection of who we are as people and professionals. Therefore, we think that it's important that you understand something about us and the perspectives we bring individually and collectively to this book.

Our Background and Experience

Both of us are advocates for children and adolescents who, for a variety of reasons, may be regarded as at risk of educational failure or disengagement. Each of us has taken on professional roles specifically to improve the educational experiences and future prospects of these young people. These roles have included classroom teacher, director of educational programming, teacher educator, program developer, dropout prevention coordinator, worksite supervisor, project evaluator, and executive director. Ultimately our desire to advocate for students considered at risk pushed us to find and secure resources to sustain initiatives that would lead to greater student empowerment and achievement—socially, civically, emotionally, economically, intellectually, and academically. We want to equip other like-minded practitioners with the tools and strategies that will help them to secure and to sustain grants that will make a difference for all children and adolescents.

The Need to Write Grants

You can do this! But the truth is that education practitioners have to write grants to support the initiatives that make a difference in the lives of children, families, and communities. There's no way around it. We live in a time when general funding for educational initiatives is being constricted, reduced, or eliminated. Increasingly, the financial support necessary to develop small- and large-scale initiatives is coming from grant-funded sources, including the government, private foundations, and corporate sponsors. Educators are fundamentally doing good work. But the resources and political climate needed to support this work in public schools have been compromised over the last several years, making schools progressively more dependent on bringing in additional funds from outside sources and in need of practical strategies to promote sustainability. One of our purposes in writing this book is to help educators more successfully secure grants and manage projects through basic knowledge, good advice, and practical tools that will ultimately benefit students, their schools, and communities.

The Need to Collaborate

You can do this! But to be successful you *must* collaborate with other people. Significant community issues such as youth violence, teen pregnancy, illiteracy, and drug and alcohol abuse typically have multiple and intertwined causes and effects that cannot be addressed by one group or multiple groups of educators working independently. Joint efforts founded on collaboration and partnerships are the way to address these and other complex issues and to meet the needs of your school community. We believe, based on years of experience, that virtually all educational projects are strengthened to the degree that they build working partnerships with other organizations or individuals with common interests and distinct resources to bring to the table.

Partnerships also strengthen the crucial connection between school and community. From a grantor's perspective, there is strong and growing interest in funding collaborative projects as opposed to efforts proposed by a single organization or an individual. The people with the money recognize the value of pooling resources, time, and effort within a community to achieve a vision not otherwise possible when entities work alone. We devote the last chapter to the principles and practices of collaboration in the hope that practitioners will better understand the interdependent connection between building true partnerships and long-term sustainability of effective programs.

An Overview of the Book

The first part of the book is all about knowing what you need to know, and doing what you

need to do, to secure grant funding for your project. In Chapter 1 we introduce you to the language of grants, help you to understand different kinds of grants and who sponsors them, and acquaint you with the Request for Proposals (RFP)—the framework for most grant applications.

Once you are familiar with "grant speak," we delve into how to clearly define your project idea and the needs it addresses in Chapter 2. We show you how to make a case for your needs with data, and we provide resources for locating grant makers whose priorities and interests match yours.

Chapter 3 is filled with suggestions on how to put together a winning proposal. Each element of the RFP is outlined, and we suggest who should write it and in what order. We also recommend how to put your grant application package together as a cohesive whole and how to incorporate the comments and biases of actual funders and grant makers.

Before you mail your application package, read Chapter 4, which provides an inside perspective on what happens to your proposal when it gets to the funder. We explain the process for reviewing proposals, provide sample scoring rubrics, and present strategies for how to make a positive and lasting impression on the reviewers.

The second half of the book focuses on establishing the systems and structures that your project needs to be successful. Beginning in Chapter 5, we guide you through the critical steps you need to take immediately after learning you have been awarded a grant. Priority activities, such as negotiating your budget, developing a media plan, and establishing an effective management structure, are described.

Project success and sustainability is intricately linked with authentic assessment of project activities and outcomes. In Chapter 6 we provide you with a detailed explanation of how you can evaluate your project. We show you how to identify the intended uses and users of the evaluation, identify a lead evaluator, and develop clear (measurable and observable) outcomes and indicators of success. Common and accessible data collection tools, methods, and strategies are described.

The last chapter focuses exclusively on the inseparable link between the long-term viability of your project and collaboration. Most of us at one time or another have thrown around the term collaboration, but its real meaning can be hard to grasp. To achieve sustainability, project leaders need to develop a common understanding of collaboration and gauge the extent to which their partnerships are as healthy and productive as they could be. Chapter 7 demonstrates how to do just that.

The World of Grants:
Surveying the Landscape

So you want to write a grant. Or maybe you don't want to write a grant, but you and your colleagues have determined that this is the best route to making an essential project happen. If you haven't written a grant before, the process can appear quite intimidating from the outside. Maybe you've heard horror stories about how you need to spend months figuring out the grant landscape, its language and procedures, before even starting to write a proposal. Or maybe you've heard that common refrain of grant writers: "We never really had much of a shot at getting it, considering the number of applicants."

In some circles, grant writing has developed its own mystique. We want to debunk this notion that you need a master's degree in grant writing. If you have common sense, time, and energy, you can write a successful grant proposal. The first step for a new grant writer is believing that you can do this!

Approach writing a grant much as you would approach applying for a job, an experience we've all had. Let's say you're going after a teaching position. You check out the field to see who's hiring in your specialty area in the districts or communities where you're willing to work. You identify an opportunity that you want to pursue. To get the job, you need to know as much as you can about the school and the district you are applying to. Do they share your values and educational philosophy? Are they a good match? You need to put together a cover letter and a résumé that best represent who you are and that align with the job description. You want your application information to be written clearly and organized in a way that's easy to follow and interpret. You make the case that they obviously want you for the job, not someone else who may appear on paper to be equally qualified. And, just in case you don't get selected for this job, you send your application packet, with minor adaptations, to a few other districts that look like a good, if not ideal, match.

Now consider this. You want to secure funding to start a new program in your school district—let's say an after-school education program for underperforming students. You do a little research on similar programs, how these are funded, and who's doing the funding. You check out the organizations that seem to be interested in supporting this kind of work. Which one seems best aligned with your goals for the project? Where's the right match? You develop an application for funding that clearly articulates your need, the design for your project, and how you will demonstrate and measure success. You want your project to stand out as the best at addressing the funder's priorities, using the basic guidelines provided. And, just in case this funder doesn't select your project, you send your proposal to a few others, adapted to follow the guidelines provided by each.

Writing a good grant is a lot like applying for a job—in both cases, you want to present yourself clearly and effectively as *the* best

choice. In each case, an interview may be in order before the selection is made. In essence, the processes are similar and straightforward. Use the resources, ideas, and information in this chapter and in Chapters 2 through 4 to help you navigate the grant development process to increase your prospects for being selected as *the* best candidate. You can do this!

Grant Terminology: Reading the Signs

You can't travel far down the grant-writing road if you can't read the signs. Just as in education, law, and health care, the world of grant writing has its own jargon. So let's begin our journey into the land of grants by learning to speak the basic language.

What exactly do we mean by a *grant*? A grant is the actual money or other resources provided to carry out a specific project. A grant is the prize or reward, if you will, that you go after to support a project that you want to bring to fruition. Grants are provided by organizations or agencies that are interested in making specific kinds of initiatives happen and that have the resources to do it. Usually these organizations or agencies award grants through a competitive process, meaning that people apply, their application packages are reviewed, and only the best proposals get grants.

The funds that are given to support winning projects are often referred to as *grant awards.* The actual grant award specifies the amount of the grant being given and the period for using grant funds. Grant awards often come with lists of other specific criteria relating to the use of the funds provided.

As in the job-seeking scenario, someone pursuing a grant is an *applicant.* You may be applying for a grant as an individual, or on behalf of the educational authority you represent, or (more typically) on behalf of a partnership working together to find and secure funding for a project. As an applicant you follow a true application process, which is determined by the organization or agency with the grant money.

The organizations or agencies that are providing grants are called a number of different things: *grantor, funder,* or *grant maker* are all terms that represent their role in the process. We use these terms interchangeably throughout the book. Grantors may be federal or state government agencies or departments, or foundations that represent corporations or private organizations.

The grant information that you submit to a potential funder is in the form of a *proposal* or *application.* These terms are also interchangeable in relation to the grants process. Grant proposals usually consist of a common set of components that detail the who, what, where, when, how, and why of your project. The proposal usually also includes a budget for supporting the work to be done and a description of how you will measure success.

A proposal describes your intended project in some detail and makes the case for why it should be funded.

Last, but certainly not least, your proposal is most commonly written in response to a *Request for Proposals,* or *RFP* (or less commonly, a *Request for Applications,* or *RFA).* This is the invitation by a grantor to submit an application or proposal to receive funding. We discuss RFPs in detail later in this chapter.

Types of Funders

Grants are grants are grants. In every case, a grant is about people following a process whereby they tell someone else why they should be awarded money to carry out a project of some kind. But what the process entails, how the case is made, and the types of projects that can be funded vary from one grantor or funder to another. Here's a brief overview of the primary types of funders you may wish to pursue.

Federal Funders

Within the United States government are 26 agencies, departments, bureaus, and offices that issue grants that relate in some way to their area of jurisdiction. Most grant funds are also authorized by legislation passed by Congress as a way of supporting action under these laws. For example, through the U.S. Department of Education, specific grant projects related to the delivery of vocational and technical education are authorized by the Carl D. Perkins Vocational and Technical Education Act.

Federal grants tend to be fairly complex and bureaucratic because of their legislative roots and all of the regulation that accompanies this process. Most of these grants, such as the Safe Schools/Healthy Students or 21st Century Community Learning Center initiatives, are also highly competitive. It is not uncommon to be directly competing with several hundred other applicants from across the country. On the plus side, many federal grants are sizable compared with most grants available through other sources (millions of dollars over the long term versus a much lower dollar figure over a short period of time).

For education and social service projects, most relevant grant opportunities come out of the Department of Education, the Department of Health and Human Services, the Department of Justice, and the Department of Labor. The federal government, however, also supports specific programs within agencies that you might not immediately think of that can fund work in different areas. The Department of Transportation, for example, has funding that could support educational projects related to effectively getting students where they need to go. Keep an open mind about the possibilities for funding across a variety of agencies seemingly unrelated to your area of interest.

The federal government also awards grant funds focused more specifically on certain types of activities. Grants for education, for example, fall into several categories:

- ❑ *Research grants* intended to "systematically inquire and examine"
- ❑ *Demonstration grants* intended to "pilot or demonstrate good ideas"
- ❑ *Training grants* aimed at providing "targeted skills instruction and education"
- ❑ *Dissemination grants* that support the "sharing of best practices"
- ❑ *Planning grants* to support "project preparation and development"
- ❑ *Curriculum development grants* typically used to "create teaching and instructional materials"

Because the demonstration grant is the type most commonly sought by educators, and because the application for a demonstration grant tends to be the most extensive and comprehensive (and by its very nature encompasses nearly all elements that any type of grantor might request), we use it to provide examples throughout the book.

State Funders

In many ways, state grants mirror federal grants, though usually with less bureaucratic complexity. The process does vary by state and by program area, however, and some grant recipients report having greater reporting and monitoring responsibilities for their state grants than for federal awards. Many state grant programs are also essentially pass-throughs for federal funding. For example, Eisenhower and Goals 2000 funds are block grants to the states from the U.S. Department of Education. The state education agencies in turn issue RFPs to subgrant these funds to local school districts and communities that submit winning project proposals. For example, block grants were awarded by the Vermont Department of Education to four school districts to establish career academies at local high schools.

One potential advantage to pursuing state grants is that the potential competition is, by geographic definition, considerably less than for federal grant projects. Thus, your odds for winning state-level grants are generally better than for federal grants, but the dollar total for state grants is also usually smaller.

Local Funders

Many city or other municipal governments also have the capacity and resources to award grants to support good work in their communities. Some of these funds (for example, some community and economic development funds that can be used for a wide range of projects) originate with the federal or state government and again are subgranted locally. The parallel continues with local versus state grants, as with state versus federal. The grants tend to be less competitive as the geographic area shrinks, and the dollar amounts are also smaller.

The more local the grant, the easier it is to establish personal relationships with the funding agency. Therefore, you and your *project partners* (the individuals and organizations that are strategically aligned with and supportive of your project) can more easily communicate with each other and the funder. This close relationship also creates opportunities to engage local funders directly in your project activities, such as kick-offs and celebrations, local media events, classroom presentations, student mentoring, or worksite learning experiences. This partnering relationship can lead to the funder becoming a real advocate for long-term monetary support for your project.

Local funders also include small foundations and corporations who only support projects in your area. Many communities throughout the country, for example, have established a *community foundation*—an organization specifically set up to collect and disburse funds to address local needs.

Private Foundation Funders

Private foundations are everywhere. The 2003 Annual Report of the Foundation Center identifies 76,682 private foundations operating across the United States, with member profiles representing 360,000 grant opportunities. These foundations are often established by wealthy *philanthropists* (individuals who commit personal resources for the common good), their families, or their financial managers. Private foundations vary widely in their interests as well as the size of their giving. Some award hundreds of dollars per year in local community grants; some award millions per year through several different program areas across the country. (For example, Bill and Melinda Gates are high-profile philanthropists whose foundation has awarded millions of dollars to support high school reform initiatives.)

Researching what's available is an important first step to accessing private foundations. In Chapter 2 we provide a number of resources and recommendations for doing so. Private foundations, particularly smaller ones that provide grants in a limited geographic area, sometimes have idiosyncratic operations. Grant decisions may be made by a board of trustees or similar group that includes members of the donor's family or close associates. It's wise to research the nature of an organization's true interests and how decisions are made before submitting a proposal. A good match can pay off with long-term support from a real ally.

Corporate Foundation Funders

A corporate foundation is a somewhat independent grant-making organization that is linked to the company that established it. The foundation is a way for the corporation to demonstrate its public goodwill by providing cash (and sometimes other company resources) to causes that it chooses to support. Areas of support also sometimes relate to the nature of the company's business. A primary interest of the Verizon Foundation, for example, relates to integrating technology and technology education. The Ben & Jerry's Foundation has a fundamental interest in grassroots social change initiatives related to their mission of operating as a socially responsible corporation.

The grant application and grant-reporting processes for corporate foundations tend to be considerably less complex and bureaucratic than those for federal, state, and local grants. These processes also vary from one foundation to another, and sometimes vary by the size of grants awarded. Still, the nature of these processes can be one significant consideration when deciding which grant sources to pursue.

Keep in mind that these organizations often restrict their giving to the communities in which they operate. There are exceptions; some large corporations award grants nationally but still favor projects in "their" communities. Corporate foundations often establish points of contact by assigning people within their local operations to oversee or manage the activities of the foundation and to make sure that they are appropriately matching up with effective local organizations and partnerships. For corporations in your area that have a foundation and that have education or social services as an interest, these are good people to get to know. Figure 1.1 summarizes the types of funders or funding categories.

A Word About Politics

The amount of money available through grants from public sources (federal, state, or local) is subject to the political priorities of those in

1.1 Types of Funders

FUNDING CATEGORY	DESCRIPTION	OPPORTUNITIES	LIMITATIONS
Federal	U.S. government grants 26 agencies, six award types	Big funding awards Involvement in a large-scale initiative with national implications	Lots of bureaucracy Extensive application process High degree of competition
State	State government grants Often "pass-throughs" for federal grants	Geographically targeted Less competitive	Some bureaucracy Extensive application process
Local	City or municipal grants	Less competitive Strong potential for community collaboration	Awards often limited in scale
Private	Thousands of organizations across the United States Often established by philanthropists	Possibility of sizable awards In comparison, far less bureaucratic	So many to choose from and pick through Idiosyncratic in operations
Corporate	Independent grant maker affiliated with parent company	Possibility of sizable awards Usually straightforward and simple application process	Funding priorities often limited Grants often targeted at specific communities with corporate interests

power. The level of funding available through private sources (private and corporate foundations) tends to be somewhat more dependent on the economic health of the sponsoring organization. Foundation funding is generally stronger during economic boom times (when the stock market is doing well) and weaker when the economy is not doing as well. The economic and political climate affects grant making. In restricted or conservative times, you may need to submit a proposal application to a wider range of funders to increase your chances of getting an award.

A Closer Look at the Request for Proposals (RFP)

The most common abbreviation of the grant world is *RFP*, which stands for Request for Proposals. This is the funder's invitation to you to "ask me for the money" or "show me your project." Almost all grant awards, the funds provided in response to a good proposal, begin with a careful analysis of an RFP. The RFP provides the guidelines for all the information you need to include in your proposal to be considered for funding. It also specifies deadlines for submitting your proposal and delivery instructions. It may include formatting specifications for writing your proposal (such as margin width, line spacing, font size), attachments required (such as letters of support, staff résumés, promotional materials, fiscal reports), and other essential information.

Most RFPs contain a typical set of components, though the RFP from any organization will have its own unique features. Nearly all funders will want answers to these questions:

❑ What is the project idea? How does it relate to your mission? To ours?

❑ Why is this project important, or what needs will it address?

❑ What are the goals of the project? What outcomes are expected?

❑ What are the activities that you will undertake to reach your goals?

❑ How will you know if you are being successful? What measures will you use?

❑ What will the project cost? How much do you need from us?

❑ Who else is supporting the project and how are they supporting it?

❑ Who are the key individuals and partners that will carry out the project? What are their qualifications and experience?

❑ If successful, how will you continue to support the project in the long run?

In Chapter 3 we describe each RFP element, in which the above questions are threaded, in much more detail. For now, we want to acquaint you with two examples of RFPs. The first is an example of a federal RFP for the Mentoring Program in the Department of Education's Office of Safe and Drug-Free Schools. It is shown in two parts. Figure 1.2 describes the absolute priorities of the grant, eligibility requirements of applicants, and the selection criteria; and Figure 1.3 provides the application format and guidelines.

Following the figures, a summarized RFP from a corporate sponsor (the Allstate Foundation) is described; it stands in stark contrast to its federal counterpart.

Allstate offers grants in three areas—safe and vital communities; tolerance, inclusion and diversity; and economic empowerment.

1.2 Sample Federal RFP Notice of Award and Selection Criteria

30794   Federal Register / Vol. 69, No. 104 / Friday, May 28, 2004 / Notices

DEPARTMENT OF EDUCATION

RIN 1865–ZA00

Office of Safe and Drug-Free Schools—Mentoring Programs

AGENCY: Office of Safe and Drug-Free Schools, Department of Education.

ACTION: Notice of final priorities, requirements, and selection criteria under the Mentoring Program.

SUMMARY: The Deputy Under Secretary for Safe and Drug-Free Schools announces final priorities, requirements, and selection criteria under the Mentoring Program. The Deputy Under Secretary will use these priorities, requirements, and selection criteria for a competition in FY 2004 and may use them in later years.

DATES: *Effective Date:* These priorities are effective July 7, 2004.

FOR FURTHER INFORMATION CONTACT: Earl Myers, U.S. Department of Education, 400 Maryland Avenue, SW., room 3E254, Washington, DC 20202–6450. Telephone: (202) 708–8846. E-mail address: *earl.myers@ed.gov,* or

Bryan Williams, U.S. Department of Education, 400 Maryland Avenue, SW., room 3E259, Washington, DC 20202–6450. Telephone: (202) 260–2391. E-mail address: *bryan.williams@ed.gov.*

If you use a telecommunications device for the deaf (TDD), you may call the Federal Information Relay Service (FIRS) at 1–800–877–8339.

Individuals with disabilities may obtain this document in an alternative format (*e.g.,* Braille, large print, audiotape, or computer diskette) on request to the contact persons listed under **FOR FURTHER INFORMATION CONTACT.**

SUPPLEMENTARY INFORMATION: We published a notice of proposed priorities, requirements, and selection criteria for this program in the **Federal Register** on March 15, 2004 (69 FR 12138).

In response to the comments received, this notice of final priorities, requirements, and selection criteria contains significant changes from the notice of proposed priorities. We have revised the proposed definition of school-based mentoring; added a new factor to the selection criterion "Quality of the Project Design" and revised the point distribution within that criterion; and changed the proposed Application Requirement for community-based organizations. We fully explain these changes in the Appendix—Analysis of Comments and Changes found elsewhere in this notice.

Note: This notice does not solicit applications. In any year in which we choose to use these final priorities, requirements, and selection criteria, we invite applications through a notice in the **Federal Register**. A notice inviting applications for new awards under this program for FY 2004 is published elsewhere in this issue of the **Federal Register**.

Absolute Priority

This priority supports projects that address the academic and social needs of children with the greatest need through school-based mentoring programs and activities and provide these students with mentors. These programs and activities must serve children with the greatest need in one or more grades 4 through 8 living in rural areas, high-crime areas, or troubled home environments, or who attend schools with violence problems.

Competitive Preference Priority

We will award five additional points to a consortium of eligible applicants that includes either: (a) At least one local educational agency (LEA) and at least one community-based organization (CBO) that is not a school and that provides services to youth and families in the community; or (b) at least one private school that qualifies as a nonprofit CBO and at least one other CBO that is not a school, and that provides services to youth and families in the community.

The consortium must designate one member of the group to apply for the grant, unless the consortium is itself eligible as a partnership between a LEA and a nonprofit CBO.

To receive this competitive preference, the applicant must clearly identify the agencies that comprise the consortium and must include a detailed plan of their working relationship and of the activities that each member will perform, including a project budget that reflects the contractual disbursements to the members of the consortium. For the purpose of this priority, a "consortium" means a group application in accordance with the provisions of 34 CFR 75.127 through 75.129.

Eligibility Requirements for All Applicants

To be eligible for funding, an applicant must include in its application an assurance that it will: (1) Establish clear, measurable performance goals; and (2) collect and report to the Department data related to the established Government Performance and Results Act (GPRA) performance indicators for the Mentoring Programs grant competition. We will reject any

application that does not contain this assurance.

Application Requirements for CBOs

To be eligible for funding, each CBO must include in its application an assurance that: (a) It is an eligible applicant under the definitions provided in the application package; (b) timely and meaningful consultation with an LEA or private school has taken place during the design and/or development of the proposed program; (c) LEA or private school staff will participate in the identification and referral of students to the CBO's proposed program; and (d) the LEA or private school will participate in the collection of data related to the established GPRA performance measures for the Mentoring Programs grant competition.

Definitions

(1) The term "school-based mentoring" means mentoring activities that are closely coordinated with schools, including involving teachers, counselors, and other school staff in the identification and referral of students, and that are focused on improved academic achievement, reduced student referrals for disciplinary reasons, increased bonding to school, and positive youth development. (2) The term "core academic subjects" means English, reading or language arts, mathematics, science, foreign languages, civics and government, economics, arts, history, and geography.

Performance Measures

We have identified the following key GPRA performance measures for assessing the effectiveness of this program: (1) The percentage of student/mentor matches that are sustained for a period of twelve months will increase; (2) The percentage of mentored students who demonstrate improvement in core academic subjects as measured by grade point average after 12 months will increase; and (3) The percentage of mentored students who have unexcused absences from school will decrease.

Selection Criteria

The Deputy Under Secretary will use the following selection criteria to evaluate applications under this competition. The maximum score for all of these criteria is 100 points. The maximum score for each criterion is indicated in parentheses.

(1) *Need for the Project.* (10 points) In determining the need for the proposed project, the following factor is considered:

1.2 Sample Federal RFP Notice of Award and Selection Criteria *continued*

The magnitude and severity of problems that will be addressed by the project, including the number of youth to be served who: (i) Are at risk of educational failure or dropping out of school, (ii) are involved in criminal, delinquent, or gang activities, or (iii) lack strong, positive role models. (10 points)

(2) *Quality of the Project Design*. (30 points)

In determining the quality of the design of the proposed project, the following factors are considered:

(a) The degree to which the applicant proposes a high-quality mentoring project that provides for, but is not limited to: (1) A low student-to-mentor ratio (one-to-one, where practicable), (2) frequent contacts between mentors and the children they mentor; and (3) mentoring relationships of 12 months or more duration. (10 points)

(b) The quality of mentoring services that will be provided, including the quality of services designed to improve academic achievement in core academic subjects, strengthen school bonding (*i.e.*, positive commitment and attachment to school), and promote pro-social norms and behaviors, and the resources, if any, that the eligible entity will dedicate to providing children with opportunities for job training or postsecondary education. (5 points)

(c) The capability of each eligible entity to implement its mentoring program effectively, and the degree to which parents, teachers, community-based organizations, and the local community have participated, or will participate, in the design and implementation of the proposed mentoring project. (5 points)

(d) The extent to which the design of the proposed project includes a thorough, high-quality review of the relevant literature, including new research, a high-quality plan for project implementation, and the use of appropriate methodological tools to ensure successful achievement of project objectives. (10 points)

(3) *Quality of the Management Plan*. (35 points)

In determining the quality of the management plan, the following factors are considered:

(a) The quality of the system that will be used to manage and monitor mentor reference checks, including, at a minimum, child and domestic abuse record checks and criminal background checks. (10 points)

(b) The quality of the training that will be provided to mentors, including orientation, follow-up, and support of each match between mentor and child. (10 points)

(c) The quality of the applicant's plan to recruit and retain mentors, including outreach, criteria for recruiting mentors, terminating unsuccessful matches, and replacing mentors, if necessary. (5 points)

(d) The extent to which the applicant provides a comprehensive plan to match mentors with students, based on the needs of the children, including criteria for matches, and the extent to which teachers, counselors, and other school staff are involved. (5 points)

(e) The extent to which the applicant demonstrates the ability to carefully monitor and support the mentoring matches, including terminating matches when necessary and reassigning students to new mentors, and the degree to which the mentoring program will continue to serve children from the 9th grade through graduation from secondary school, as needed. (5 points)

(4) *Quality of Project Personnel*. (10 points)

In determining the quality of project personnel, the Secretary considers:

The qualifications and relevant training of key staff, including time commitments, and experience in mentoring services and case management. (10 points)

(5) *Quality of the Project Evaluation*. (15 points)

In determining the quality of the evaluation, the following factors are considered:

(a) The extent to which the methods of evaluation will provide performance feedback to the Department, grantees, and mentors, and permit periodic assessment of progress toward achieving intended outcomes, including the GPRA performance measures for the Mentoring Programs grant competition. (5 points)

(b) The extent to which the methods of evaluation include the use of objective performance measures that are clearly related to the intended outcomes of the project and will produce quantitative and qualitative data on the GPRA performance measures for the Mentoring Programs grant competition. (10 points)

Executive Order 12866

This notice of final priorities, requirements, and selection criteria has been reviewed in accordance with Executive Order 12866. Under the terms of the order, we have assessed the potential costs and benefits of this regulatory action.

The potential costs associated with the notice of final priorities, requirements, and selection criteria are those resulting from statutory requirements and those we have determined as necessary for

administering this program effectively and efficiently.

In assessing the potential costs and benefits—both quantitative and qualitative—of this notice of final priorities, requirements, definitions, and selection criteria we have determined that the benefits of the final priorities justify the costs.

We summarized the costs and benefits in the notice of proposed priorities, requirements, and selection criteria.

Intergovernmental Review

This program is subject to Executive Order 12372 and the regulations in 34 CFR Part 79. One of the objectives of the Executive order is to foster an intergovernmental partnership and a strengthened federalism. The Executive order relies on processes developed by State and local governments for coordination and review of proposed Federal financial assistance.

This document provides early notification of our specific plans and actions for this program.

Applicable Regulations: 34 CFR parts 74, 75, 77, 79, 80, 81, 82, 84, 85, 86, 97, 98, 99 and 299.

Note: The regulations in 34 CFR Part 86 apply to institutions of higher education only.

Electronic Access To This Document

You may view this document, as well as all other documents of this Department published in the **Federal Register**, in text or Adobe Portable Document Format (PDF) on the Internet at the following site: *http://www.ed.gov/ news/fedregister.*

To use PDF you must have Adobe Acrobat Reader, which is available free at this site. If you have questions about using PDF, call the U.S. Government Printing Office (GPO) toll free at 1–888– 293–6498; or in the Washington, DC, area at (202) 512–1530.

You may also view this document in text or PDF at the following site: *http://www.ed.gov/programs/ dvpmentoring/applicant.html.*

Note: The official version of this document is the document published in the **Federal Register**. Free Internet access to the official edition of the **Federal Register** and the Code of Federal Regulations is available on GPO Access at: *http://www.gpoaccess.gov/nara/ index.html.*

(Catalog of Federal Domestic Assistance Number: 84.184B Office of Safe and Drug-Free Schools—Mentoring Programs)

Program Authority: 20 U.S.C. 7140.

1.3 Sample Federal RFP Application Format and Guidelines

Application Format

Unless you plan to submit electronically, applicants are required to submit one original application (with all signatures signed in black ink) and two copies (unbound). In addition, applicants are requested, but not required, to submit one additional copy for a total of four. All pages should have printing on only one side and must be numbered, including any appendices. Do not attach anything to the application that cannot be photocopied using an automatic process, e.g., anything stapled, folded, pasted, or in a size other than 8 1/2 x 11 inches on white paper.

A complete application comprises the following items in the order specified:

1) **ED Form 424.** ED Form 424 must be completed in accordance with the instructions provided.

2) **Project Abstract.** The project abstract should be limited to 200 words, providing an overview of the proposed project, **including the number of students to be served.** The applicant's name (as shown in item 1 of ED Form 424) and title (as shown in item 13 of the same form) should be clearly marked.

3) **Table of Contents.** The table of contents should identify the page number for each of the major sections of the application, in addition to any appendices.

4) **ED Form 524 and Budget Narrative.** Please follow the instructions contained in ED Form 524 for completing the budget. Please note that the appropriate column on Form 524 must be completed for each year that funds are requested (up to 3 years). Failure to supply a budget and a narrative for each project year will result in no funding for those years.

A detailed budget narrative is also required to explain the information provided in ED Form 524. Using the same budget categories provided on ED Form 524, the narrative should provide sufficient detail for reviewers to easily understand how project costs for each year were determined.

Please explain the basis used to calculate indirect cost rates, including evidence of a negotiated indirect cost rate, as well as certain costs for travel, supplies, and contractual, or any other costs that may appear unusual.

All applicants must budget for annual attendance for the project director and one other staff person at the annual 3-day Office of Safe and Drug-Free Schools National Conference, and any other training the Secretary may require. For planning purposes applicants may assume one person attending three training sessions each year. All meetings will take place in Washington, DC.

5) **Application Narrative.** Describe your proposed project in detail with particular attention to all selection criteria and statutory requirements, and provide a description of all aspects of the project. The program narrative section should not exceed 25 double-spaced pages using a standard font no smaller than 12-pt, with 1-inch margins (top, bottom, left, and right). The narrative should be succinct and well organized, following the format and sequence of the selection criteria. If you fail to address all the

1.3 Sample Federal RFP Application Format and Guidelines continued

selection criteria, including each weighted sub-element, our experience suggests your application will not score well enough to be funded.

6) Program Specific Assurances. Please see "Assurances."

7) Assurances, Certifications, and Disclosure. These forms must be reviewed and signed by the individual identified in item 15 (a) of ED Form 424. Failure to submit the signed assurances, certifications, and disclosure will delay any possible award. The following assurances, certifications, and disclosure forms are included in this application package:

> Standard Form 424B - Assurances – Non-Construction Programs;
>
> ED Form 80-0013 - Certifications Regarding Lobbying; Debarment, Suspension, and Other Responsibility Matters; and Drug-Free Workplace Requirements;
>
> ED Form 80-0014 - Certification Regarding Debarment, Suspension, Ineligibility and Voluntary Exclusion – Lower Tier Covered Transactions;
>
> Standard Form LLL - Disclosure of Lobbying Activities (*note: this form is not required if there are no lobbying activities to disclose*).
>
> GEPA 427 Statement. Please see "Application Requirements."

APPLICATION SUBMISSION GUIDELINES

Attention Electronic Applicants: Please note that you must follow the Application Procedures as described in the Federal Register notice announcing the grant competition.

- Some programs may require electronic submission of applications, and those programs will have specific requirements and waiver instructions in the Federal Register notice.
- If you want to apply for a grant and be considered for funding, you must meet the following deadline requirements.

Applications Submitted Electronically

You must submit your grant application through the Internet using the software provided on the e-Grants Web site (http://e-grants.ed.gov) by 4:30 p.m. (Washington, DC time) on the application deadline date. The regular hours of operation of the e-Grants website are 6:00 a.m. Monday until 7:00 p.m. Wednesday; and 6:00 a.m. Thursday until midnight Saturday (Washington, DC time).

Please note that the system is unavailable on Sundays, and after 7:00 p.m. on Wednesdays for maintenance (Washington, DC time). Any modifications to these hours are posted on the e-Grants Web site.

If you submit your application through the Internet via the e-Grants Web site, you will receive an automatic acknowledgment when we receive your application.

1.3 Sample Federal RFP Application Format and Guidelines continued

Note: Applications may only be submitted electronically via the e-APPLICATION system. Applications sent via electronic mail will not be accepted.

Applications Sent by Mail
You must mail the original and two copies of the application on or before the deadline date to:

U.S. Department of Education
Application Control Center
Attention: CFDA #84.184B,
Washington, DC 20202

To help expedite our review of your application, we would appreciate your voluntarily including one additional copy of your application.

You must show one of the following as proof of mailing:
- A legibly dated U.S. Postal Service Postmark.
- A legible mail receipt with the date of mailing stamped by the U.S. Postal Service.
- A dated shipping label, invoice, or receipt from a commercial carrier.
- Any other proof of mailing acceptable to the Secretary.
- If you mail an application through the U.S. Postal Service, we do not accept either of the following as proof of mailing:
    - A private metered postmark.
    - A mail receipt that is not dated by the U.S. Postal Services.

An applicant should note that the U.S. Postal Service does not uniformly provide a dated postmark. Before relying on this method, an applicant should check with its local post office.

Special Note: Due to recent disruptions to normal mail delivery, the Department encourages you to consider using an alternative delivery method (for example, a commercial carrier, such as Federal Express or United Parcel Service; U.S. Postal Service Express Mail; or a courier service) to transmit your application for this competition to the Department. If you use an alternative delivery method, please obtain the appropriate proof of mailing under "Applications Sent by Mail," then follow the instructions for "Applications Delivered by Hand."

Applications Delivered by Hand
You or your courier must hand deliver the original and number of copies requested of the application by 4:30 p.m. (Washington, DC time) on or before the deadline date to:

1.3 Sample Federal RFP Application Format and Guidelines *continued*

U.S. Department of Education Application Control Center
Attention: CFDA #84.184B
550 12th Street, SW, PCP - Room 7067
Washington, DC 20202

To help expedite our review of your application, we would appreciate your voluntarily *including one additional copy of your application*

The Application Control Center accepts application deliveries daily between 8:00 a.m. **and 4:30 p.m. (Washington, DC time), except Saturdays, Sundays and Federal holidays.**

If you send your application by mail or if you or your courier delivers it by hand, the Application Control Center will mail a Grant Application Receipt Acknowledgment to you. If you do not receive the notification of application receipt within 5 days from the mailing of the application, you should call the U.S. Department of Education Application Control Center at (202) 245-6288.

You must indicate on the envelope and—if not provided by the Department—in Item 4 of the Application for Federal Education Assistance (ED 424 (exp. 11/30/2004)) the CFDA number—and suffix letter, if any—of the competition under which you are submitting your application.

If your application is late, we will notify you that we will not consider the application.

Retrieved from http://www.ed.gov/fund/grant/apply/grantapps/index.html

According to Allstate's Web site (see http://www.allstate.com/community for the full RFP) proposals should contain the following information:

❑ Cover letter

❑ A summary of the grant request

❑ Brief description of how the proposed program or project relates to the current focus areas, of The Allstate Foundation

❑ A timetable for project implementation

❑ Brief statement of the organization's history, mission, goals, service area, and constituents

❑ A budget for the proposed project

❑ An audited financial statement from the previous year

❑ A copy of the most recent annual report

❑ A copy of the nonprofit status exemption letter from the IRS

❑ List of the officers and board members

❑ List of other donors

A comparison of the two RFPs reveals a great deal of variation in format. You can see, however, that ultimately both are requesting the same type of information (as opposed to volume of information). These examples provide some initial insight into the kinds of details provided by funders to help you, the applicant, shape your request for grant funds. We showcase them in this chapter as an orientation to what the grant application process, from the funder's perspective, requires in its entirety. Just scan them quickly to familiarize yourself with the sections and the required elements. Don't get bogged down in the details.

The RFP in Figure 1.2 and the accompanying guidelines presented in Figure 1.3 are typical documents in the federal grant application process. Even a brief read through the RFP and the guidelines can be exhausting! What we hope you gleaned from a scan of Figures 1.2 and 1.3 is that the federal grant application process does require the completion of multiple forms, sections, and assurances, but none of these requirements is particularly unclear—just time consuming. For this reason, it is essential that you plan to prepare a federal RFP application package well ahead of the submission deadline.

Federal grant applications are very detailed and must comply with the regulatory requirements attached to the legislation that authorized the particular grant funds in question. The rules that govern the issuing of federal grants are generally far more extensive than those associated with private or corporate foundations. You can see the density of details in the federal RFP compared with the RFP of the corporate funder. In a similar way, state grants often need to conform to some federal as well as state regulatory requirements.

Foundation grant requests vary a great deal in complexity. The Allstate example is a fairly simple and straightforward list of elements required for the proposal. Although the government and foundation RFPs are quite different, they have common elements that reflect the funder's need to understand the nature of the project, how it relates to the organizational goals and mission of both the applicant and the funder, how it will be funded, the fiscal and personnel qualifications of the applicant, and so forth.

KEY POINTS TO REMEMBER

❑ Grant writing is a straightforward and *doable* process that you can accomplish successfully.

❑ Understanding the basic terminology of grants is important for moving forward.

❑ Grant funders may be federal, state, or local agencies; private foundations; or corporate foundations.

❑ Understanding the distinctions among the potential funders is important when deciding where to apply.

❑ The RFP is at the heart of the grant development process, and all RFPs have a few common elements.

Preparing to Write Your Grant Proposal

2

Now that you've decided to take up the challenge of writing a grant proposal, don't let your determination waver. Go for it! You have a sense of the grant landscape, recognize the different types of grantors available to you, and are familiar with general RFP requirements and variability. Now it is time to prepare to write. Make no bones about it—*preparing* to write the proposal is as important as actually *writing* it. Before you sit down with a grantor's application package, you need to develop a strong idea for your project design, cultivate collaboration with partners, clarify the need for your project, make the case for the need with data, and find at least one funder whose priorities and interests match those of your project. In this chapter we discuss each of these steps in preparing to write your grant proposal and provide general sources to locate potential funders. Remember, you can do this! As Mary Hall (1988) says, "There is no special mystique about proposal writing. Anyone with a good, well-planned idea, appropriate research on sources of support, and the ability to communicate in writing can do a successful job of preparing a funding request" (p. 2).

Develop a Strong Idea for Your Project Design

Although it may be obvious that you need an idea in order to pursue a grant to fund it, it's worth taking the time to be clear about the idea so that you can present it succinctly to partners and funders. In formulating your idea, you may want to consider a number of questions.

Questions to Ask

Who will benefit from this project? If the project is to create a new alternative education program, for example, which students or youth will it directly benefit? Are there other beneficiaries such as parents and guardians, teachers, the local social service network, the school district?

What is the basic purpose or function of the project? Is the project intended primarily to improve teaching skills and strategies? To provide new learning opportunities for students in the community? To expand support services for students with special needs? To create a partnership with area post-secondary schools? Whatever the purpose is, articulating it is essential.

What is the geographic area to be served? Is the project confined within your school district? Does it involve a partnership with neighboring districts? Is the project defined by a service region (for example, a labor market region defined by the Department of Labor or a state human services region)? It's important to decide the boundaries for those who will participate in your project.

What is the outcome that you envision? Do you know what effect you want to have on the community, and can you anticipate an end result? Is the outcome in the form of a written

product, a new facility, a more engaged faculty, students achieving at higher levels, new working relationships among area employers and schools?

These are just a few of the prompts that may help you to define your idea and be able to share it with others. You can also think about your project idea in ways related to how the idea originated. What situation motivated you to think about such a project in the first place?

Sources of Ideas

You could *invent an idea* for a local project to address an identified need in a unique way. New project ideas can take the form of a *pilot project,* whereby applicants approach funders with a new idea whose value and effectiveness they hope to successfully demonstrate after initial implementation for a specified period. Some funders encourage this approach with designated funding for pilot projects. Rich came up with an idea for a program called the Career Leaders Academy to increase the leadership skills and career preparation of high school juniors and seniors. It built naturally on career development and community-based learning programs already established and coordinated by Linking Learning to Life, the nonprofit organization for which he works. At the same time the program was new in that it focuses on leadership skills, it brings students together from across area high schools, and it provides for peer mentoring by the junior and senior "career leaders" who work with students in 7th through 10th grade. With organizational partners, he pursued funding for the idea from a foundation that was particularly interested in providing *seed money,* or start-up funds for new programs.

Another source of a project idea can be the *adaptation* of an existing project or program. With this approach you are essentially borrowing some components of an effective model in place and significantly adding to or modifying it to match your concept and needs. Rebecca worked with a school district that had designed a new dropout prevention program that incorporated career exploration and peer mentoring for 8th graders. The Parallel Academic Support Services program was very successful, and the district decided to develop a similar program or adaptation for its 9th graders that was tailored to their developmental readiness. With her teacher colleagues, she sought and received grant monies to adapt the existing 8th grade delivery model for the 9th grade.

Your idea may also essentially be a *replication,* or copy, of a good thing (a curriculum, a professional development program, a research project, a governance structure, or a student services program) that's already working well somewhere else and that matches an identified need in your school and community. An example of this approach is the D.A.R.E. program. D.A.R.E., which stands for Drug Abuse Resistance Education, is a curriculum-based program intended to give kids the life skills they need to avoid involvement with drugs, gangs, and violence. The program was started in Los Angeles in 1983 and has since grown across the nation. Local individuals have accessed a variety of grant funds to get it up and running in their schools and communities.

Many grant writers and project developers get stuck because they believe they should come up with a new or seemingly original idea. The reality is that someone else is probably already implementing a version of your idea somewhere else. It is often a much better use of time to research and adapt projects that seem to align with your basic idea than to start from scratch. Regardless of the source of your project idea, carefully define the who, what, why, how, when, and where of your initiative.

Cultivate Collaboration with Partners

A project idea may originate with a single individual, but if it remains that person's idea alone throughout the project development and grant writing phases, certain negative consequences may result. Namely, the commitment to it, the likelihood of funding, the possibility of effective implementation, and the long-term sustainability of the idea are greatly diminished. To the greatest extent possible, you should build and nurture commitment to the project idea among multiple people and organizations. This means that the idea itself will likely change somewhat to reflect multiple institutional and personal values, but the incorporation of additional perspectives will strengthen it. As the original "owner" of the idea, you need to be willing and able to "let it go and let it grow" by engaging others in pursuing the initial idea further.

Building shared ownership and partner involvement right from the start can have a significant payoff when it's time to implement the funded project. It's important to note that grantors now increasingly look for collaboration as a key ingredient of effective projects and ones that they want to invest in. More and more frequently, RFPs ask applicants to list their collaborators, the collaborators' qualifications, the specific roles each will play, the matching resources partners bring, and their commitment to sustaining the project.

Rich drafted a *concept paper,* or initial description of the idea, for the Career Leaders Academy described earlier and took it to organizational staff and board members for review and revision. He also brought it to the principals of three area high schools and to members of the local chamber of commerce. Individuals from each group provided input on the project design. The concept paper retained the core idea, but Rich made several additions that further defined both the program and the needs it addressed. The schools and the chamber wrote strong letters of support to submit with an initial concept proposal to a regional foundation. The foundation responded favorably to the initial idea and was impressed with the collaborative nature of the project, which included shared ownership and support.

Clarify the Need for Your Project

A need must drive your idea for a grant request. You should be able to show what community need your project addresses and that your project can, in fact, do something to effectively address it. If your idea focuses on providing preschool programs to children of single working parents, but no single working parents live in your area (which means no need exists), no grantor would see the value in funding it. Similarly, if your idea calls for the development of a bullying prevention program for 6th graders, but physical violence is rampant throughout all grade levels in the district (the need is overwhelming), potential grantors will question the ability of your project to make a real difference.

As you define project needs, consider the following questions (adapted from Hall, 1988):

❑ What specific community needs are addressed and for whom?

❑ Why should these particular needs and this specific population receive attention at this time?

❑ If your particular project is not implemented now, what will happen?

❑ Who else is working on these needs, either locally, regionally, or nationally? What have they learned that is applicable to your project? What evidence do you have that your efforts do not unnecessarily duplicate those of others?

❑ Is the need really solvable? Can your project really address the needs you have identified? What evidence do you have that your program can really make a difference?

❑ Is the need a priority in your organization's strategic plan?

❑ Is the need seen as especially important by those groups or organizations (partners) whose support and involvement is critical to the success of the project?

❑ What constraints or difficulties should be anticipated in meeting the need?

True story: In 2002, the Youth Outreach Unit of a Missouri police department received a $273,000 state grant to support their project idea intended to "battle Goth culture." As it turned out, no Goth-influenced youth could be located in the area, and in April 2004, after spending $141,000 to set up the program, $132,000 was returned to the state funding agency (Harper's Index, August 2004). Moral of the story: Research the need for your great idea!

Make the Case for the Need with Data

The vast majority of competitive educational grant funds are provided to help fill gaps or meet needs that cannot adequately be addressed with existing public resources (at least according to the funder's perspective). Therefore, a critical element in convincing funders to invest in you is to make the need you're addressing compelling and clear. You can do this in a few different ways.

Presenting the Facts

You must have data from your own community, or from whatever geographic area your project encompasses, that demonstrates a need that matches the interests of the potential funder. Some grant writers make the mistake of writing long, elaborate descriptions about the woes of their target group without providing quantifiable evidence of the problem. Essentially you want good data to do most of the talking.

Let's take an example. The federal government issues a project RFP that seeks new initiatives to increase the high school completion rate in communities experiencing significant problems related to school dropouts. Through data collected from local school districts and the state department of education, you are able to show a 69 percent high school completion rate for the Middletown School District, a seemingly low figure. If you can then compare this with a 75 percent completion rate in the nearby Bondville District and an 81 percent rate in adjacent Sunny Valley, you begin to build your case. If you can then compare Middletown's rate with a 79 percent rate statewide and a 77 percent rate nationwide, your case becomes stronger.

If you follow up with information from human service agencies that shows, for example, comparatively high rates of unemployment among 16- to 24-year-olds, a higher than average percentage of adults in the community without college degrees, average household incomes below the federal poverty level, and high rates of substance abuse among 18- to 21-year-olds, your case becomes even more compelling. Most funders want tangible, quantifiable evidence of the need.

Another way to make your case is through individual vignettes or case studies that tell the stories of individuals who exemplify the need in a personal way. These examples can reach the emotive side of proposal readers, but they usually don't carry the weight of numerical or quantitative data. The case can be made that you can find a few equally needy examples in virtually any community, but a few examples can't illustrate the depth of the need.

Finding Data to Make Your Case

Good data are essential for an effective description of your need. Here are some places to look for information that can help make your case.

School and District Data. State and federal law requires school districts to collect and report on a broad array of data related to student demographics and outcomes, educator qualifications and tenure, financial indicators, and more. Most of this information is in the *public domain,* meaning that anyone can have access to it. School districts generally host their own Web sites that you can easily access, but the information posted by districts varies tremendously. Districts also produce annual reports or "school report cards" that summarize educational and fiscal results for the district. Individual school Web sites usually provide site-level demographic and assessment data and often link to other pertinent sources for information that could be used to establish need.

Community Data. You may also seek out more general information regarding your local community. For example, in building the needs statement for your project you may want to reference a host of indicators related to the overall health and well-being of the community. You can contact local city or municipal government offices to inquire if they have recently published reports of this nature that summarize data across multiple community measures. Using the increased search capabilities of the Internet, you can often identify several excellent sources of community data by simply using the name of your community and words such as *information* or *data* in an Internet search.

Statewide Data. State governments collect a tremendous range of information. Often the best community-wide data are available through state agencies that collect common information for all communities throughout the state. The state department of education has responsibility for collecting information from all schools and districts (and in some cases, institutions of higher education as well) and summarizing many different data sets. The department's Web site is usually a rich source for this information either directly or through multiple links. As an added benefit, this information is often presented in a format that allows for comparison against other schools or districts statewide, as well as against statewide averages.

In a similar way, you can access other important data sets through other state agencies or departments. The state human services agency collects information related to poverty levels, substance abuse, child and infant health measures, incarceration and recidivism, teen pregnancy, and many other topics. The state department of labor gathers data regarding levels of unemployment, youth unemployment, wage earnings, job retention, and other information related to individual labor markets, or local economic activity zones.

Other departments may also have statewide and local data relevant to your project. The information provided by these sources can help build a powerful needs statement for your project backed by real data.

National Data. Many kinds and sources of data are available on the national level. Rather than listing a variety of agencies and organizations with their own data sets, we recommend starting with the National Center for Education Statistics, which is the primary federal entity for collecting and analyzing data related to education in the United States and other nations. It is a rich source for information across multiple content areas and can be accessed at http://nces.ed.gov/.

Find a Funder Whose Priorities and Interests Match Those of Your Project

Now that you have a sense of what your project is really about, the need it meets, and how it will positively affect your community, you need to find the funders whose interests and priorities align with yours. This matching process is an essential step in ultimately getting the money to carry out your project.

Let's take a minute to look at how funders articulate their funding priorities. Federal grant projects clearly describe the grant program priorities in a common format that always appears as part of the RFP published in the *Federal Register.* Private and corporate foundations usually provide a concise definition of their philanthropic interests, which are important to know before writing an application that will likely draw their attention. Concrete examples in which funders describe

2.1 Notice of Award Invitation with Funder Interests and Priorities

---

DEPARTMENT OF EDUCATION

Office of Safe and Drug-Free Schools—Partnerships in Character Education
Notice Inviting Applications for New Awards for Fiscal Year (FY) 2004
Catalog of Federal Domestic Assistance (CFDA) Number: 84.215V

Purpose of Program: Under this program we provide Federal financial assistance to eligible entities to assist them in designing and implementing character education programs that take into consideration the view of parents, students, students with disabilities (including those with mental or physical disabilities) and other members of the community, including members of private and nonprofit organizations.

Priorities: This competition includes one absolute priority and one invitational priority that are explained in the following paragraphs.

To be considered for funding, each applicant must address the absolute priority.

Absolute Priority—The design and implementation of character education programs that:

(A) Are able to be integrated into classroom instruction and to be consistent with State academic content standards; and
(B) Are able to be carried out in conjunction with other educational reform efforts.
Within this absolute priority, we are particularly interested in applications that address the following invitational priority.

Invitational Priority—Experimental and Quasi-Experimental Evaluation Designs

The Secretary is particularly interested in receiving applications that propose evaluation plans that are based on rigorous scientifically based research methods to assess the effectiveness of a particular intervention. The Secretary intends that this priority will allow program participants and the Department to determine whether the project produces meaningful effects on student achievement or teacher performance.

Retreived from http://www.ed.gov/legislation/FedRegister/announcements/2004-1/022404e.pdf

their particular interests and priorities are most illustrative. Figure 2.1 is an example from the federal Department of Education for a large demonstration grant competition focused on building partnerships in character education.

As you can see in this example of a federal grant, priorities are expressed in two ways. An *absolute priority* must be addressed directly by any applicant. Secondarily, this notice of award competition invites applicants to also consider taking on an *invitational priority* related to project evaluation. Federal projects often include a much longer and more detailed list of priority interests to address in order to compete for funding within a particular program area. Here are two examples of priority interests of Department of Education programs (all of which are accessible at http://www.ed.gov):

Program Title: Jacob K. Javits Gifted and Talented Student Education. The purpose of the Javits program is to carry out a coordinated program of scientifically based research, demonstration projects, innovative strategies, and similar activities designed to build and enhance the ability of elementary and secondary schools to meet the special education needs of gifted and talented students. The major emphasis of the program is on serving students traditionally underrepresented in gifted and talented programs, particularly economically disadvantaged, limited English proficient, and disabled students, to help reduce the serious gap in achievement among certain groups of students at the highest levels of achievement. Grants are awarded under two priorities. Priority One supports initiatives to develop and scale-up models serving students who are underrepresented in gifted and talented programs. Priority Two supports state and local efforts to improve services for gifted and talented students.

Program Title: Assistive Technology State Grant Program, AT State Grant Technical Assistance. The AT State grant program supports consumer-driven state projects to improve access to assistive technology devices and services. The goal is to eliminate programmatic, policy, and other barriers that preclude or prevent persons with disabilities from acquiring the assistive technology devices and services they need. The Technical Assistance program provides technical assistance, through grants, contracts, or cooperative agreements, on a competitive basis to individuals, service providers, states, protection and advocacy entities, and others.

Corporate or private funders also articulate their interests clearly. One example is the General Electric Foundation, which funds several educational priorities. GE Foundation priorities are first defined broadly, for the organization as a whole, and then in terms of the organization's interest in education; this is followed by further detail in several different educational program areas. (See GE's Web site at http://www.ge.com/foundation/grant_initiatives/education.html for more details.)

Paying close attention to the priorities and interests of a funder is a critical part of the grant development process. As the government and corporate examples illustrate, funders' interests vary, and the way they articulate their interests is also quite different. Take the time to understand the distinct priorities of any funder you choose to pursue. If it's unclear from a funder's written information whether or not your project is a close match, contact the funder and ask. This small investment of time up front can determine whether or not a much larger time commitment devoted to grant development and writing is appropriate with that particular grantor.

Now that you have developed your project idea, articulated the needs that your project addresses, and gained a sense of how funders express their interests, you just need to find the right matches. There are, indeed, many ways and places to look for grant funding opportunities. In this section we point out some of the key places to begin your search, particularly if you are new to grant searching. We provide direct Web links for ease of access. In general, you should regard these as starting points that can and will lead you to many others as you become more familiar with what's out there. Ultimately you can develop mechanisms that deliver grant sources to you. As a case in point, neither of us uses open grant searches much any more because we have developed links, personal connections, and other mechanisms that result in grant information being sent directly to us on a regular basis. We also discuss some of these mechanisms at the end of this chapter.

Staying Informed

Lots of people (just like you) are submitting grant proposals (similar to yours) to funders (like the ones you've identified). To be competitive you have to stay informed about who is funding, what they are funding, and when they are funding it. Whatever you do, don't wait for a funding source to find you. According to Donald Orlich (2002), cited in ASCD's March 2003 *Education Update,*

> If a school waits to find out about a grant from a general mailing or word of mouth, it won't have time to prepare a proposal, says Donald Orlich, author of the ASCD book *Designing Successful Grant Proposals.* "Monitoring is the most important aspect because it helps a school make the match and be aware of the deadline. You don't want to be caught racing to a deadline . . . if you don't have the information, you can't do the preparation." (Allen, 2003, p. 3)

School districts and individual schools can subscribe to periodic newsletters, such as *Grants for K–12* (Quinlan Publishing) that announce grant application deadlines for federal, state, corporate, and private funders and provide background information on organizations and agencies that sponsor grant competitions. You can also visit helpful Internet sites that provide regularly updated information on a wide variety of grant competitions (see the end of this chapter for a list of sites and descriptions of their services).

Keeping Your Options Open

It's also important to remember to be open to all possible funding opportunities when you are exploring funders to pursue. You never know who shares your priorities and interests. Hall (1988) effectively makes this point:

> Many proposal writers are too narrowly focused when they enter this search. They think, "Well, if it is a science project, obviously we should approach the National Science Foundation." But perhaps the project's approach involves new

methodology for training technicians (an idea that may appeal to some corporations), or it is intended to benefit students from disadvantaged backgrounds (a mission of many foundations, corporations, or other private sector donors), or the project's success may benefit the economy in a particular locale (thus qualifying for sources with a special interest in that geography or the state's economic development agency). (p. 31)

Open-mindedness and creativity in thinking about who might want to support your project opens up a broader range of possible sources of grant funding.

Take Advantage of Sources to Find Funders

Here are some good starting points for finding potential grantors for your project. Each is identified with a Web site for ease of access. The first group consists of overall sources of grant information; the second group is more specific to education.

General Sources

Federal Grants Information. A relatively new comprehensive online source for searching for grants through all federal agencies and departments is located at http://www.grants.gov. This site enables you, as a potential grant applicant, to look at all of the grant offerings available through the federal government and to use different search criteria (such as period of grant release, categories of interest) to refine

your search to match the nature of your project. A word of caution: Do not define your search criteria too narrowly or you may miss related opportunities.

The Foundation Center. This source has compiled a tremendous amount of information on foundations; the site offers a range of free and pay search options. http://fdncenter.org

Grantionary. The Grantionary is a list of grant-related terms and their definitions. http://www.eduplace.com/grants/help/grantionary.html

GuideStar. This site provides financial data, including IRS tax filings, on foundations and charities. It also offers a searchable database and pay search options. http://www.guidestar.org

Philanthropy News Digest. This weekly news service of the Foundation Center is a compendium, in digest form, of philanthropy-related articles and features culled from print and electronic media outlets nationwide. http://fdncenter.org/pnd/

Education-Specific Sources

Department of Education Forecast of Funding Opportunities. This document lists virtually all programs and competitions under which the Department of Education has invited applications for new awards, as well as those they plan to announce at a later date. It provides actual or estimated deadline dates for the transmittal of applications under these programs. The lists are in the form of charts organized according to the department's principal program offices. Note: This document is advisory only and is not an official application notice of the Department of Education. http://www.ed.gov/fund/grant/find/edlite-forecast.html

The Forecast of Funding Opportunities is one of several helpful links available on the Grants and Contracts page of the Department of Education Web site. Other links provide access to documents such as "Grantmaking at ED: Answers to Your Questions About the Discretionary Grants Process." http://www.ed.gov/funding.html

Education World Grants Center. This site is updated regularly with a "featured grant" and a listing of other current grants. It also provides tips and resources for grant writers. http://www.education-world.com/a_admin/archives/grants.shtml

Eduref.org. This online directory, developed by education librarians, has a page on grants that links to various grant-related sites and to reports, articles, and online communities for grant writers. http://www.eduref.org/cgi-bin/res.cgi/Educational_Management/Grants

eSchool News School Funding Center. This site provides up-to-the-minute information on grant programs, funding sources, and technology funding. http://www.eschoolnews.com/resources/funding/

FastWEB. FastWEB is the largest online scholarship search available, with 600,000 scholarships representing more than one billion scholarship dollars. It provides students with accurate, regularly updated information on scholarships, grants, and fellowships suited to their goals and qualifications, all at no cost to the student. Students should be advised that FastWEB sells student information (such as name, address, e-mail address, date of birth, gender, and country of citizenship) collected through their site. http://www.fastweb.com/

Federal Resources for Educational Excellence (FREE). More than 30 federal agencies formed a working group in 1997 to make hundreds of federally supported teaching and learning resources easier to find. The result of that work is the FREE Web site. http://www.ed.gov/free/

Fundsnet Online Services. This is a comprehensive Web site dedicated to providing nonprofit organizations, colleges, and universities with information on financial resources available on the Internet. http://www.fundsnetservices.com/

GrantsAlert. GrantsAlert is a Web site that helps nonprofits, especially those involved in education, secure the funds they need to continue their important work. http://www.grantsalert.com/

Grant Writing Tips. SchoolGrants has compiled an excellent set of tips for those who need help in developing grant proposals. http://www.schoolgrants.org/tips.htm

Healthy Youth! Funding Resources. This Web page, part of a site maintained by the

National Center for Chronic Disease Prevention and Health Promotion, provides a link to a Healthy Youth Funding Database. The database contains information about funding opportunities for adolescent and school health programs from both federal agencies and private organizations. http://www.cdc.gov/healthyyouth/funding/index.htm

School Funding Center. The School Funding Center is dedicated to helping schools find every funding source available to them in the United States. A paid subscription is required in order to access the center's entire grant database. http://www.schoolfunding-center.com/index.asp

School Grants. This is a collection of resources and tips to help K–12 educators apply for and obtain special grants for a variety of projects. http://www.schoolgrants.org

Get Grant Information Delivered to You

Once you get immersed in finding and accessing good grant information, you'll appreciate having that information delivered directly to you. Here are a few mechanisms that can make that happen.

SPIN Search is a pay service offered by InfoEd International (http://www.infoed.org) that provides information on grant opportunities, including grantor contact information, program descriptions, eligibility criteria, geographic restrictions, and range of awards. The site sends this information directly to your e-mail address once you have identified your areas of interest and selected keywords to define your searches. Although this is a pay service, your district or organization (or a partner organization) may have a membership that you can use to get good grant information.

At www.grants.gov, the comprehensive federal grant source mentioned earlier, you have the option of setting up a free e-mail service. You can indicate the granting agencies and types of grants that interest you. The site will send you information on federal grant listings that match your criteria whenever new postings are made to the site.

The Internet has many topical interest area listservers that you can subscribe to for free and that include grant information. An example is PEN NewsBlast (http://public-education.org); in addition to providing education news stories, it offers information on specific grant opportunities and links to general sources (including many of those we mentioned earlier) in each issue. NCSET News (http://www.ncset.org/enews/default.asp), from the National Center on Secondary Education and Transition, provides information specific to students with disabilities, including grant opportunities, upcoming events, and published resources. Consult your colleagues and professional associations to find other sources that can be directed your way.

KEY POINTS TO REMEMBER

❑ The project idea is the foundation for your proposal; it can represent a new concept or replicate an effective existing program or practice.

❑ Your project should clearly address a community need. Use quality data to support the identified need.

❑ Funders articulate their interests and priorities for soliciting grants. Carefully matching your project idea and addressed needs with their interests and priorities will lead to the best funding prospects.

❑ You can access a wealth of grant information sources online. Some sources allow you to arrange for direct, regular delivery of information.

Writing a Successful Proposal:
Tips and Tools

So you have a potential funder in mind, the needs your project addresses match the priorities of the grantor, and you have begun to forge partnerships with others to make your initiative a reality. Now it is time to begin writing. Most requests for proposals and grant application packages have a common set of components, though the order and titling of these vary to some degree. Completing an application—that is, writing a successful proposal—includes paying careful attention to each element and writing directly in response to the guidelines for that section provided by that particular funder or grantor. This may sound obvious, but funders repeatedly lament that the vast majority of proposals they receive do not provide the information they requested in the place it's supposed to be.

Debbie Rey, who supervises the office that processes proposals for the W. K. Kellogg Foundation, reports that 80 percent of the grant applications that cross her desk are immediately rejected. According to her, the reason that so many don't pass muster is that the applicants didn't do their legwork: "They may have glanced at the Web site but didn't dig deeper to learn Kellogg's specific grant-making priorities" ("Grant Makers Reveal," 2003).

"Your request should be crystal clear and showcase how projects fit perfectly within funders' priorities," says Karen Murrell, senior director of outreach and education for the Fannie Mae Foundation. "Do research. Fannie Mae rejects most proposals immediately because they fall outside its funding priorities" (CD Publications, 2003).

Read a Funded Grant Proposal

One simple recommendation, particularly for those new to grant writing, is to find a good (that is, funded) proposal and read it thoroughly. And here's an important tip: Read it alongside the RFP that it was written in response to. Comparing each heading in the RFP with the actual response from a successful applicant can be extremely valuable.

Obviously, doing this exercise with more than one grant proposal and RFP will increase your knowledge of what grant reviewers think is good. It will also give you some comparative information regarding aspects such as writing tone, how data are used, how the applicant organizations articulate their strategic match with funders' priorities, examples of management and partnership structures, how budgets are constructed in relation to the project design, and so forth.

How do you get your hands on examples of good proposals? Talk to colleagues or organizational partners about grants that they have been awarded and ask to review these. Contact educators from other districts who have been awarded grants similar to the ones you seek. Most people are willing to share samples of their success as long as they do not see you as a direct competitor for the same funding sources. Some grants competitions provide copies of winning proposals as exemplars. If you find a grant program that relates to the kind of project you would like to receive

funding for, contact the funder and request copies of successful proposals. You also can locate (usually online) other projects that were funded by the grantor or the RFP that you have identified. Contact the successful applicants and ask for a copy of their application package. When a local district with whom Rebecca worked was seeking a 21st Century Community Learning Center grant, she obtained a copy of a successful 21st Century grant application from colleagues in the district where she was formally employed. Most people are more than willing to share this information because they already have the money and will not see you as competition.

Avoid Blind Submissions: Build a Relationship with the Funder

It's simple human nature to want to be supportive of the people you know and like. This basic principle can also play out in the process of applying for and securing support from your "friends" who represent federal or state agencies and corporate or private foundations. Establishing a personal connection to someone representing the funding source can have a positive result when grant award decisions are ultimately made.

Another way to think about the concept of building a relationship with a particular funder is to ask yourself, How can my proposal stand out from the possibly hundreds of others that are similar when it comes down to making the tough choices? One answer is that if the grants officer, board trustee, or other individual engaged in the review process knows something about you—your integrity, your qualifications and experience, your commitment to truly making a difference to your community, your thoroughness in addressing the interests of the funding agency—then you and your project can rise out of the heap of good proposals.

As a matter of policy, we no longer submit a proposal to a potential funder without first making some kind of personal contact. You should do the same, using any of a variety of approaches. A simple one is to call or e-mail an identified grants officer responsible for the grant program you are interested in. (Calling is better than e-mailing because it is more personal and allows you to more easily express interest and enthusiasm.) Read the RFP carefully and research the funder, looking for such things as examples of past giving, levels of grant awards and geographic distribution, current priorities, and the language they use to articulate their interests. Use this information to develop intelligent questions that relate your project idea to their RFP. Make sure to provide your name and the name of your organization and repeat it at the end of your e-mail or phone conversation. If you have the opportunity, mention who some of your partners are. Demonstrate your commitment to collaboratively meeting a real need.

Another way to build a personal link is to ask a grants officer or other funder representative if he or she would be willing to review a basic concept draft of your project. The intent is to give you constructive feedback on your project, but perhaps more important, *you directly engage the funder in the development of your project.* In a sense you become partners in the creation of the project and the subsequent proposal. Funders are more likely to support a project that they actually helped to create to meet their interests and criteria. Private and corporate foundations generally have more flexibility in their ability to develop personal links, but all grants programs, including federal and state agencies, are managed by people who want to make a difference.

Understand the Elements of an RFP

Figure 3.1 provides a standard list of common RFP elements in the order that they appear in most grant application packages. RFP elements refer to the concepts that you have to address, section by section, in a grant application package. The language that funders use to specify different elements is not always consistent, so we have provided the most common and universally accepted descriptions for each RFP element.

In the chart we make recommendations regarding who should take primary responsibility for writing each element.

3.1 RFP Elements

ELEMENT	DESCRIPTION	PERSON RESPONSIBLE	ORDER OF PREPARATION	OTHER SUGGESTIONS/TIPS
Title Page	Title of project, name of project director, complete contact information, lead organization, dates of project, budget request, and signature of applicant.	Project director	Near last, when budget numbers are final	Title page varies by type of funder. Make sure that you have the correct CFDA* number for federal/state awards and correct organizational ID numbers (e.g., federal tax ID number) requested.
Abstract	More common with state and federal grants. Brief summary that clearly articulates the purpose, objectives, need, success measures, and results. Typically a stand-alone paragraph or two.	Project director/lead proposal writer	Last	Think of this as the published description of your project. Does it describe the project clearly and include the critical points? Think short and simple.
Statement of Purpose	Succinct description of the goals and objectives of the project and expected outcomes, with link to bigger-picture significance.	Lead proposal writer	First	Be sure that your purpose clearly matches the funder's stated priorities.
Vision and Mission Statements	Vision statement—an outward look at the idealized impact of the initiative. Mission statement—an inward look at the project and how it operates in ideal terms.	Lead proposal writer with partner input	First	Some RFPs request vision and mission statements in lieu of statements of purpose. If they exist and it makes sense to do so, incorporate the mission and vision statements already created by the lead agency and partner organizations.
Statement of Need	Well-documented description of the problem the project addresses. Clear use of data to support the case that your project is necessary, timely, and significant.	Lead proposal writer	Second	Use facts and quotes, but don't tell a sob story! Grant makers want to fund a winner, not a whiner. Be clear about the problem and what needs to be changed. (See Chapter 2.)

*Catalog of Federal Domestic Assistance (CFDA) numbers are assigned to all grants offered by the federal government.

3.1 RFP Elements *continued*

Element	Description	Person Responsible	Order of Preparation	Other Suggestions/Tips
Project Design	Alternatively referred to as Project Approach/Action Plan/Procedures. A plan of action that includes all the activities you will carry out, and in what sequence, that is aligned with your objectives and that will be delivered to meet the needs you have identified. A description of what you are doing, with whom, where, and when.	Lead proposal writer with partner input	Third	Show that you have carefully thought this through. The design elements will likely change when you actually do the project, but you need to have a clear initial plan. It is wise to incorporate any research or literature that supports the choices you have made in your project design.
Management Plan	Time line for how your project design will unfold and organizational chart showing the relationship between project personnel and project responsibilities.	Lead proposal writer with partner input	Fourth	Use an organizational management flow chart (such as a Gantt chart). Convince the readers of your proposal that you are tightly organized to run the project but won't do it in isolation. The structure needs to include methods for true partner engagement in decision making. (See Chapter 5.)
Evaluation Plan	Description of how you will observe/measure progress and outcomes; plans for types of data to be collected, instruments to be used, process for data analysis, and how results will be used and reported.	Lead evaluator with partner input	Near the beginning and thereafter, as goals and objectives are being developed	Ideally, the plan should include both qualitative and quantitative data collection methods. Be clear about how the evaluation plan aligns with project goals and objectives. Evaluation should be formative and summative in nature. (See Chapter 6.)

3.1 *RFP Elements* continued

Element	Description	Person Responsible	Order of Preparation	Other Suggestions/Tips
Dissemination Plan	Description of how you will promote and market the project and share evaluation findings internally and externally. Details the type of reports you intend to create for the funder. Also includes presentations at appropriate conferences.	Lead proposal writer with partner input	Fifth	Describe how you will use all of the PR/promotional vehicles available through all of your partners—Web sites, newsletters, media links—to get the word out. Have at least one media or PR partner with the expertise to develop your marketing efforts.
Project Personnel—Qualifications	Demonstration of the ability of the organization and its partners to successfully carry out the project; list of key staff and their responsibilities (with résumés) and partner or consultant roles.	Lead proposal writer	After the management plan is clear	Emphasize the qualifications of the project director. This may not be the role to assign to someone "looking to go full time" or running out of funding from an earlier project. Competitively speaking, you want the right person with compelling qualifications.
Budget	Delineation of project costs, with narrative that breaks down calculations and rationale for each line item; may require demonstration of matching sources of funding that support the project. Addresses the amount of money to be contributed by the lead organization and the amount and type of support from partner organizations.	Lead agency submitting grant (with fiscal agent if different from lead agency)	Sixth	Budget must align with project need and design. Make sure all your requested budget items are allowable costs.

3.1 RFP Elements *continued*

ELEMENT	DESCRIPTION	PERSON RESPONSIBLE	ORDER OF PREPARATION	OTHER SUGGESTIONS/TIPS
Plan for Sustainability	Indication of the actions you will take and resources available to you (including matching funds) that will increase the likelihood that the initiative will become an integrated part of the community and be supported by it in the long run.	Project director and lead grant writer	Near last	Sustainability is not something you go out and get—it is something you build from the get-go. (See Chapter 7.) Sometimes a plan for sustainability is requested in the Budget or Qualifications sections.
Attachments	Documents that vary according to the nature of the project and sponsoring agency; may include letters of support, audit or other financial information, résumés of personnel, promotional materials, IRS tax determination letter.	Designated administrative staff person to collect	Near the beginning and thereafter, with frequent revisions	Make a clear list of what's needed at the start and assign someone to gather the documents. Some of these may take time to collect, especially from partners. If letters of support are needed, be prepared to draft some of these for others to sign. Don't throw in every nifty-looking document related to your project. Include only what illuminates the essentials of the initiative. (See Chapter 4.)

See Figure 3.1 for the tasks the following people are responsible for:

❑ Lead proposal writer—the "official" grant writer; this could be the project director, but could easily be someone else

❑ Project director (if identified)

❑ Lead agency—the fiscal entity that will be responsible for administering the grant

❑ Lead evaluator—the internal or external person responsible for program evaluation

❑ Project partners—personnel from other organizations contributing in some way to the project

❑ Administrative staff—support personnel working with the lead proposal writer

We also recommend the order in which you should tackle each section. The order of writing is important. You will have to curb your desire to complete the sections that appear to be simple or short (such as the abstract) just to gain a sense of completion. Completing the sections in our suggested order intuitively makes sense and will likely save you a considerable amount of time and energy.

In the final column we provide additional tips for successfully crafting your grant proposal that correspond with each element.

Put It All Together

In addition to attending to each element of a grant RFP, remember that in the end *the application package must come together as a cohesive whole.* It needs to make sense and be easily readable to the people who ultimately will decide if the project should be funded. (In Chapter 4 we give you a close-up picture of how reviewers perceive and assess the quality of application packages.) At a recent Vermont Funders Forum, a panel of grant makers talked about what they like to see in the proposals that make it to the top of their highly competitive application processes. Katherine McHugh, philanthropic director for Hemenway & Barnes in Boston and program director for Jane's Trust, advised, "Ask someone who doesn't know anything about your work to read your proposal." When you are fully absorbed in writing a grant over a period of time, with intensive work on different elements at different times, it's very difficult to see how well the final product coalesces (or does not) as a complete and meaningful whole. An objective outside perspective can provide valuable input to make sure that the proposal ultimately does come together.

In regard to the cohesiveness of a proposal, McHugh also offered this perspective:

> What's most often missing in a proposal is a discussion of "where is the organization going and how we can help you get there." . . . When I get to the end of the proposal there needs to be another paragraph or another page describing where this activity fits in addressing the issues that your mission is designed to address, and how a grant from our organization can help you advance your organizational well-

being and the cause that you care about. Try putting your request into a broader context, both at the beginning, in terms of the need, and at the end, in terms of your organizational growth; it will be very helpful to us with understanding what you care about.

Beware of Your Budget

The budget element of the RFP is often the section most unfamiliar to education practitioners. So many of us are in the business of developing ideas and putting ideas into action, not formulating viable annual budgets to support the work. The budget forms provided in application packages look pretty straightforward—just fill in the blanks for "Personnel," "Equipment," "Construction," and so forth. But beware. The budget section is scrutinized heavily in the review process, and it is essential that the money you are requesting is directly aligned with your project activities and addresses the need you have identified. Take the time necessary to determine exactly what it will cost to fund each of your project activities, each year of the grant. The worksheet in Figure 3.2 is a tool to help you determine dollar amounts for standard budget categories as they relate to your project activities.

After you've reviewed the budget format in Figure 3.2, take a look at Figure 3.3, which shows a completed budget worksheet for a summer enrichment program. A budget narrative follows the worksheet to explain in more detail how the funds were calculated in each budget category.

Follow the Directions

Why do we even bother stating such an obvious point? Because, as noted at the beginning of this chapter, funders report that the vast majority of what they get isn't what they asked for. Because sections aren't put together properly, elements aren't addressed, or sections seem to be out of order, many grant application proposals are discarded without even being read! All of the hard work that you and your partners put into grant development will come to nothing if your application is poorly assembled and doesn't make it past the first cut.

In the introduction to the book we stated our premise that we believe that you as an interested reader and educator or social service practitioner have great ideas and projects that deserve to be funded. If you want to effectively convince potential funders that this is true, remember that they are customers (much as students or parents are in your primary work). To satisfy your customers, and be rewarded for doing so, you need to attend to their needs first. Just as teachers take care of basic organizational needs in the classroom because they know that students can't learn if they are overly confused or can't find their materials, or the chapters in the books are out of order, you, the applicant, must make the conditions for reviewing your grant application ideal for the reviewer. At the most basic level, this means

3.2 Budget Worksheet

	TYPICAL BUDGET CATEGORIES	PROJECT DESIGN–YEAR ONE ACTION PLAN			YEAR ONE TOTAL COSTS
		ACTIVITY: (SPECIFY)	ACTIVITY: (SPECIFY)	ACTIVITY: (SPECIFY)	
1	Personnel (salary costs)				
2	Fringe benefits (health and life insurance, workman's compensation, FICA)				
3	Travel (air fare, mileage reimbursements)				
4	Equipment (machinery, office technology)				
5	Supplies (paper, postage, paper clips, phone, copying, etc.)				
6	Contractual costs (subcontractors, consultants)				
7	Construction (renovation and building costs)				
8	Other (allowable "other" varies by funder)				
9	**Subtotal: direct costs (lines 1–8 for each individual column)**				Subtotal: Direct Costs (all activities)
10	Indirect costs (institutional costs related to project overhead and physical infrastructure)				
11	Training stipends (nonsalary-related short-term costs)				
12	**Total costs (lines 9–11 for each individual column)**				Total Costs (all activities)

3.3 Budget Worksheet for Summer Science Academy Enrichment Program

Budget Categories	Project Design—Year One Action Plan			Year One Total Costs
	Activity: Curriculum Planning	Activity: Classroom Instruction	Activity: Field Experience	
1	Personnel (salary costs): Project Director (lead teacher), Teaching Assistant	$3,300	$5,450	$5,450	$14,200
2	Fringe benefits (health and life insurance, workman's compensation, FICA)	$1,100	$1,651	$1,651	$4,402
3	Travel (air fare, mileage reimbursements)	$72	--	--	$72
4	Equipment (machinery, office technology, large items): "Living Machine Lab4, Laptops	$8,080	--	--	$8,080
5	Supplies: copying, student materials	$500	$140	$140	$780
6	Contractual costs: stipend for field presenters	--	--	$1200	$1200
7	Construction: n/a	--	--	--	--
8	Other: student transportation to field sites, project fair	--	$425	$570	$995
9	Subtotal: direct costs (lines 1–8 for each individual column)	$13,052	$7,666	$9,011	$29,729
10	Indirect costs: grant accounting, project overhead, classroom rental	$175	$957	$288	$1,420
11	Training stipends: n/a	--	--	--	
12	Total costs (lines 9–11 for each individual column)	$13,227	$8,673	$9,299	$31,149

3.3 Budget Worksheet for Summer Science Academy Enrichment Program *continued*

Budget Narrative

Personnel: For the lead teacher, two weeks of planning, six weeks of delivery, and one week of program evaluation at $1,000 per week adds up to $9,000. For the teaching assistant, two weeks of planning and six weeks of delivery at $650 per week equals $5,200. Based on this allocation of time, approximately 23% of staff time (salary & benefit costs) is dedicated to curriculum planning and approximately 38% each to classroom instruction and field experience.

Fringe Benefits: For the lead teacher, health insurance, life insurance, FICA, FUTA, SUTA calculated at 31 percent of salary cost equals $2,790. For the teaching assistant, health insurance, life insurance, FICA, FUTA, SUTA calculated at 31 percent of salary cost equals $1,612.

Travel: Reimbursement for staff travel to and from field placement sites to plan student experience with site partners—six site visits, 32 miles each, at $.375 per mile, equals $72.

Equipment: Purchase of "living machine" lab for student classroom usage from Ocean Arks International, $3,280. Four Dell laptop computers (one for each student group to use in the classroom and in the field) at $1,200 each.

Supplies: Copying—600 copies at $.05 per copy equals $30. Binders, papers, pens, markers, calculators = $750.

Contractual costs: $200 stipends for six field presenters equals $1,200.

Other: Student transportation to field sites at $95 a day for six days equals $570. End-of-program project fair costs (room and refreshments at community center) equal $425.

Indirect costs: 20 hours of grant accounting at $35 per hour equals $700; six weeks of classroom rental at $120 per week equals $720.

following as closely as possible the instructions and guidelines provided in the RFP.

Some grants have many levels of instruction to follow. These may include format details such as the font and size of type to use, spacing in the text, size of margins, and use of page numbering. The number of copies needed and what is accepted or not accepted as attachments are frequently specified. Often RFPs include specific mailing instructions for submission of your proposal, such as deadline date for receipt or postmarking (which are different) of a mailed package, the type of carriers that can be used, whether faxed or electronic submissions are accepted, and so on. Regardless of your feelings about the worth or usefulness of these requirements, they are critical from the standpoint of whether your proposal ever gets read.

Other grant application instructions pertain to the content and meaning of RFP elements and sections. When it comes to RFP elements, again follow the guidelines and directions as closely as possible. If you have any doubt about what the funder is looking for in any particular section, contact a grants officer for clarification. The grants officer will generally appreciate your attention to detail in this regard and be happy to work with you to address your questions. This contact has the additional potential benefit of building the funder's awareness of you and your project before you submit a proposal.

Keep Bragging Rights in Context

You likely have a lot of great things to say about your project. And most proposal formats provide opportunities to do some bragging about your project, your organization, your partners, the innovativeness of your project, and how effectively it will address the identified need. But your bragging needs to be clearly within the context of the RFP—when and where the funder is asking you to accentuate the positives. As noted in Chapter 2, some grant writers work from the perspective that "if I keep telling them how great we are and what a wonderful difference we make for kids, they'll have to fund us." This does not match the reality of the vast majority of grant decisions. Funders don't like whiners and they don't like show-offs. It is your job to strike a happy medium throughout your grant application.

Submit Applications to Multiple Potential Funders

Just to be perfectly clear on this point, we don't mean that you should submit the exact same proposal to multiple sources. What we do mean is that it makes sense to take all of the focused work you have done—researching and developing an idea, articulating the need, designing a project, assessing its results, and establishing a budget for the project—and ask more than one potential funder to invest in your project.

Doing so requires carefully adapting your proposal to match the interests and guidelines of other funders. If you take a little time to research potential funders to find those that seem to match, you've already done 90 percent of the work necessary for making additional requests. You may also discover that a potential funding source is a good match for supporting a specific portion of your project, but not the whole thing. If you go for it and are successful, you have just increased your appeal to others. Funders want to see that you have successfully secured money from others, thereby decreasing their sense that the project's success or failure lies in their hands. As stated by Karen Murrell of the Fannie Mae Foundation, "Your organization's financial health should be evident. Don't ask a funder to supply your entire operating budget. Keep in mind most foundations won't be sole funders of your project" (CD Publications, 2003). And another funder, Jane Englebardt, executive director of the Hasbro Children's Foundation, said this: "When it comes to seeking grants, success breeds success. If a charity can show it has other grants, that's a plus. . . . National foundations look for organizations that are supported in their communities, so we know they're going to be strong and sustainable" (CD Publications, 2003).

The obvious advantage to this strategy is that the more potential sources you submit a proposal to, the more likely you are to successfully fund your project. Furthermore, if you get a positive response from more than one funding source, negotiating how much you will get from each for the project is a delightful problem to have. One option that may be available in this situation is to ask one funder to postpone the time frame for your award until another funder's support has expired. Many foundations in particular are willing to be flexible in this regard when they see you have a strong project that others are also willing to invest in.

KEY POINTS TO REMEMBER

❑   Take the time to read a funded grant proposal.

❑   Avoid submitting a proposal without having made personal contact with the funder.

❑   Craft each RFP element separately, but be sure all the elements come together as a cohesive whole.

❑   Follow the directions, follow the directions, follow the directions.

❑   Submit to multiple funders.

❑   Don't bank on a grant until the grant's in the bank.

4

Application Review from an Insider's Perspective

At this point in your grant-writing journey, you have been able to find a grant competition (RFP) from a funder that shares your interests and priorities. You've formed a writing team, met to clarify ideas, decided who writes which sections of the proposal, and developed a plan to get the writing done on time and with attention to quality throughout. You've gone through the nerve-racking process of writing and assembling all of the RFP elements. But before you dash off to the post office with your finished product, think carefully about the application peer review process and its ramifications for how your proposal will fare. *Make no mistake about it—the grant application peer review is the single most important event that influences whether your proposal will be funded.*

This chapter describes how your grant proposal will be handled and scrutinized through a typical application review process. We emphasize the federal demonstration grant review process, which tends to be the most all-encompassing and includes elements of most other types of grant reviews. We have had extensive experience as reviewers of grant applications made available through local, state, federal, corporate, and private sources for projects whose funding requests have ranged from $500 to $5 million. Each review process is structured a bit differently, but universal truths abound.

Peer Review

Peer review is the process through which most grant proposals are assessed within the federal and state government structures. After your proposal arrives at its destination, it is coded, copied, and collated, and then read by a panel of people. In short, individual reviewers will read your grant application, and a number of others competing for the same money, and rate it against a pre-established set of selection criteria. Then the individual reviewers meet as a full panel, discuss their ratings of each proposal, and produce an average numerical score that is used to rank each proposal against its competitors. Once your proposal has been read, rated, discussed, and ranked, the peer review process is complete, and the funding agency decides who gets funded and who does not. How your proposal fares in the peer review process is the most critical determinant of whether your proposal is funded or not.

What makes these reviewers peer *reviewers?* Reviewers are your peers in a couple of ways. First, they likely have similar professional interests as you do, and they have experience and knowledge in the type of grant for which you are applying. For example, reviewers for the Smaller Learning Communities Demonstration grant will understand the school-within-a-school model, teaming, block scheduling, and other types of smaller learning community initiatives for which you might be seeking funding. In addition, reviewers for U.S. Department of Education demonstration

grants are likely to be current or former teachers, principals, administrators, college professors, directors of nonprofits, or employees of state government social service agencies. Reviewers are also likely to have expertise in a particular field. With any grant competition, individuals with this kind of background are contacted to explore their interest and their availability to serve on a peer review panel.

What are the selection criteria? The *selection criteria* are standards that reviewers must use to evaluate the quality of your proposal. In fact, federal policy does not allow reviewers to use anything but the specific selection criteria in completing the review. The selection criteria are written in language similar to the learning standards used by classroom teachers to develop assessment rubrics. The form used to score each section of each proposal actually looks a lot like a rubric. Figure 4.1 is an example of a scoring guide for a grant competition used by reviewers to record pre-panel and post-panel scores and comments on the selection criteria. Rebecca used these rubrics when she peer-reviewed for two federal demonstration grant competitions.

Selection criteria are related to the RFP elements discussed in Chapter 3. However, the selection criteria or rubric criteria identified by grantors vary greatly depending on the agency sponsoring the competition. That said, most demonstration grant initiatives within the U.S. Department of Education use a standardized set of selection criteria that are outlined in a

4.1 A Peer Review Scoring Guide

U.S. DEPARTMENT OF EDUCATION—OFFICE OF SPECIAL EDUCATION PROGRAMS

[NAME OF COMPETITION IS INSERTED HERE, ALONG WITH THE CFDA #]

INDIVIDUAL PEER REVIEW FORM

PRINT OR TYPE	Applicant Institution: [This could be you!]	APPLICATION NUMBER XXXXX01 _____

CRITERIA	RANGE OF POINTS	INDEPENDENT (PRE-PANEL) SCORE	FINAL (POST-DISCUSSION) SCORE
1. Need for Project	0–20		
2. Quality of Project Design	0–25		
3. Quality of the Management Plan	0–10		
4. Quality of the Project Evaluation	0–20		
5. Quality of Project Personnel	0–15		
6. Adequacy of Resources	0–10		
CRITERION SCORE	0–100		

Overall Recommendation: Independent—_____   Post-Panel—_____
("A" for Approval; "D" for Disapproval)

Conditions, negotiation items, or other comments:

federal publication called EDGAR (*Education Department General Administrative Regulations*).

What does each criterion mean? The most common components on which reviewers must score your proposal are need (why is your proposed project needed?), the quality of your project design (do your activities, services, and strategies target the needs that you describe?), plan for management (is the plan clear, feasible, and appropriate?), evaluation (does the evaluation plan gather and analyze short- and long-term quantitative and qualitative data related to activities and outcomes?), quality of personnel (are all key personnel identified and qualified?), and adequacy of resources (will the facilities, supplies, and other resources support the proposed project; are the costs reasonable; and could this project be sustained in the future?).

Remember, these elements are the ones most commonly scored by reviewers. However, reviewers read every part of the application—so be sure to do a quality job in each section. (Recall that Chapter 3 provides descriptions of each component or RFP element, strategies for writing each component, and suggestions for earning the highest score possible for each element.)

How is my proposal actually scored by reviewers? Much like the criteria in a classroom rubric, each selection criterion is worth a certain number of points. For example, if the Need for the Project criterion is worth a total of 20 points, reviewers read your proposal and determine what judgments might produce a rating of 5, 10, 15, or even 20 points out of a possible 20. A typical scoring scale looks like this:

Poor	Weak	Adequate	Superior	Outstanding
0–4	5–8	9–12	13–16	17–20

Although determining the meaning of "superior" or "adequate" involves a considerable amount of subjectivity, there is an attempt to standardize the rating process (as with a rubric). For instance, a judgment of "minimally adequate" in a reviewer's mind would merit approximately half the possible points on that criterion; points would then be added or taken away from that midpoint depending on what the reviewer found to be exemplary or lacking in a proposal. Therefore, if a reviewer read the Need for the Project section of your proposal and found it to be relatively strong, he or she would start at 10 and add approximately 5 points for a score of 15 out of 20.

Are number ratings the only way my proposal will be assessed? Reviewers are reminded that the applicants actually get to see these review sheets with verbatim comments, and thus the reviewers are told (sometimes over and over) to write well and to give the applicant specific narrative feedback about strengths, and, more important, weaknesses. If your proposal is not funded, the reviewer comments should provide you with detailed information on how to improve the proposal for resubmission to future grant competitions. The proposal scoring and assessment sheet in Figure 4.2 is an example of the actual forms that grant reviewers use to record the strengths and weaknesses of each selection criterion in a proposal.

What's it like being a reviewer? Let's just say reviewers don't have much free time! Typically they're flown to Washington, D.C., or another city, put up in a hotel for four or five days, given a stack of proposals either in advance or upon arrival, and required to attend a pre-review orientation meeting with all the other people who agreed to be reviewers for a particular grant. A grant competition that generates 100 applicants likely has 40 reviewers (with 4 reviewers and 10 applications assigned to each panel).

So the reviewers have four or five days to read, write comments on, and talk about 10 proposals. That may not sound too difficult. But, in fact, the life of a reviewer (although short) is tough. How applicants write their proposals will either make the reviewer's life easier or more difficult. Remember that you, the applicant, are aiming for the former. Let's explore this a little deeper.

First, proposals aren't like typical student essays. Each proposal might be 80 pages long—50 pages of narrative and an additional 30 pages of appendix material.

Second, a quick glance through these 10 proposals reveals a wide variation in formats and writing styles. Some have headings that correspond to the selection criteria, but many do not; some have tables and figures and color graphics to break up and illustrate the narrative, but many do not; some are double-spaced and use a 12-point font that makes late-night reading easy, but many use a 10-point font and are single-spaced to get as much information as possible into the maximum allowable 40 pages of narrative.

Third, the scores that individual reviewers assign for individual proposals usually differ. Therefore, when the four reviewers come together to "panel up," it takes a great deal of time and communication skill to reach consensus. Depending on the social skills of the reviewers, the dynamics of the group as a whole, and the facilitation skills of the panel manager, discussions can range from lively and intellectually exciting to cantankerous and ill-tempered. The sheer length and variation in proposal format combined with the dynamics of communication and personality can make review work tough!

When the reviewers' work is done, they return home weary and intellectually drained, but also with an intense feeling of satisfaction (usually) from doing good work in selecting the best proposals to receive federal funding.

Increasingly, because of budget and logistical considerations, peer reviews are done by sending the proposals to reviewers across the country to read and respond to individually. In this format the "panel up" process either happens by conference call or else is elimated—in which case the grant managers in Washington (or other agency headquarter cities) compile and summarize the results.

4.2 A Proposal Scoring and Assessment Sheet

1. Need for Project (0–20 points)   Score _____

In determining the need for the proposed project, consider the following factors: (1) the magnitude or severity of the problem to be addressed by the proposed project; and (2) the extent to which specific gaps or weaknesses in services, infrastructure, or opportunities have been identified and will be addressed by the proposed project, including the nature and magnitude of those gaps and weaknesses.

Strengths:

Weaknesses:

Poor 0–4	Weak 5–8	Adequate 9–12	Superior 13–16	Outstanding 17–20

2. Quality of Project Design (0–25 points)   Score _____

In determining the quality of the design of the proposed project, consider the following factors: (1) the extent to which the design of the proposed project is appropriate to, and will successfully address, the needs of the target population or other identified needs; and (2) the extent to which goals, objectives, and outcomes to be achieved by the proposed project are clearly specified and measurable.

Strengths:

Weaknesses:

Poor 0–5	Weak 6–10	Adequate 11–15	Superior 16–20	Outstanding 21–25

4.2 A Proposal Scoring and Assessment Sheet continued

3. Quality of the Management Plan (0–10 points)   Score _____

In determining the quality of the management plan for the proposed project, consider the adequacy of the management plan to achieve the objectives of the proposed project on time and within budget, including clearly defined responsibilities, time lines, and milestones for accomplishing project tasks.

Strengths:

Weaknesses:

Poor 0–2	Weak 3–4	Adequate 5–6	Superior 7–8	Outstanding 9–10

4. Quality of the Project Evaluation (0–20 points)   Score _____

In determining the quality of the evaluation to be conducted of the proposed project, consider the following factors: (1) the extent to which the methods of evaluation include the use of objective performance measures that are clearly related to the intended outcomes of the project and will produce quantitative and qualitative data; (2) the extent to which the methods of evaluation are thorough, feasible, and appropriate to the goals, objectives, and outcomes of the proposed project; and (3) the extent to which the methods of evaluation provide for examining the effectiveness of project implementation strategies.

Strengths:

Weaknesses:

Poor 0–4	Weak 5–8	Adequate 9–12	Superior 13–16	Outstanding 17–20

4.2 A Proposal Scoring and Assessment Sheet *continued*

5. Quality of Project Personnel (0–15 points)   Score _____

In determining the quality of project personnel, consider the extent to which the applicant encourages applications for employment from persons who are members of groups that have traditionally been underrepresented based on race, color, national origin, gender, age, or disability. In addition, consider the following factors: (1) the qualifications, including relevant training and experience, of key project personnel; and (2) the qualifications, including relevant training and experience, of project consultants or subcontractors.

Strengths:

Weaknesses:

Poor 0–3	Weak 4–6	Adequate 7–9	Superior 10–12	Outstanding 13–15

6. Adequacy of Resources (0–10 points)   Score _____

In determining the adequacy of resources for the proposed project, consider the following factors: (1) the adequacy of support, including facilities, equipment, supplies, and other resources, from the applicant organization or the lead applicant organization; (2) the extent to which the budget is adequate to support the proposed project; (3) the extent to which the costs are reasonable in relation to the objectives, design, and potential significance of the proposed project; and (4) the potential for continued support of the project after federal funding ends, including, as appropriate, the demonstrated commitment of appropriate entities to this type of support.

Strengths:

Weaknesses:

Poor 0–2	Weak 3–4	Adequate 5–6	Superior 7–8	Outstanding 9–10

I know the review and scoring process can't be as logical as it sounds. What are the influential factors that I can't do anything about? It may seem strange that professional reviewers can produce quite divergent ratings on proposals whose selection criteria are relatively clear and after the reviewers have all received training on the use of these criteria. But it happens. Here are some of the most frequently occurring reasons for the discrepancies:

❑ Different reviewers on the same panel focus on different selection criteria. (For example, when we serve as peer reviewers we tend to key in on design and program evaluation.)

❑ Often one or more reviewers give a lot of credit to a proposal that introduces a wonderfully innovative, fresh solution to a problem even if the narrative is not particularly well written. These reviewers may nudge their ratings upward to give credit for this innovative idea.

❑ Similarly, one or more reviewers on a panel may give a lot of credit to proposals from applicants with a high need for resources despite a relatively poorly written proposal.

❑ Sometimes a reviewer scores a proposal more harshly or generously because he or she is familiar with the people or organization associated with the project and allows that knowledge to affect the rating in a negative or positive manner. (Federal reviewers must officially verify that they are unbiased and unaffiliated with applicants.)

❑ Some reviewers may simply not give enough time to the reviews. The ratings from these reviewers are almost always on the high side because it is much easier to write up and justify in the panel process uninformed positive ratings than uninformed negative ones.

As the applicant, you can't control how much time a reviewer has to read your proposal, but you can make your application accessible, easy to read, and thorough. By addressing each section thoroughly and creatively, you minimize inherent subjectivity in the review process.

Let's cut to the chase: Is my proposal more likely to be a winner or a loser? Remember, for each panel review only 1 of the 10 proposals, on average, can be funded, meaning that for every 1 winner there are 9 losers. The upside is that if your proposal clearly addresses each criterion and is presented in a way that makes it easy for panelists to review, you are more likely to get funded. At the very least you will receive accurate and defensible comments from the panelists who rated your proposal, and you can use those comments to improve your proposal for the next round of funding.

What does all of this information tell me about how to be more competitive when developing my grant proposal? First, write your proposal considering the reviewers' perspectives and their needs as reviewers. What does this mean?

Essentially, you have to consider two types of reviewers—those who grade easy (who give the most points to the most reasonably well-written proposals) and those who grade hard (who recognize that there can be only one or two winners and look hard to find reasons not to approve most proposals). Which of these two types of reviewers is most crucial for you to impress? Obviously the latter. If you convince the tough reviewer of your proposal's merits, then you've gone a long way to getting your proposal into the winner's circle. This is not only because your proposal will start out with a higher overall average score across all reviewers, but also because the most critical reviewers are usually the most powerful and persuasive reviewers on the panel.

So how do I impress the most critical reviewers? To do this is no different than what you have to do in a job interview or when you are trying to be an effective leader. *You need to make a positive first impression, and you need to make a positive lasting impression.* It helps to "walk a mile in their shoes"—that is, to know what reviewers are going through and make every encounter with your proposal a positive one.

The Three Impressions

A reviewer in a panel review process encounters your proposal three times: the *initial scan,* when the reviewer tries to get a feel for all the proposals and develops some initial impressions of which proposals look like winners and which look like losers; the *full individual*

review, when the reviewer reads your proposal in depth and prepares a written rating; and the *panel review process,* during which all the reviewers discuss the strengths and weaknesses of your proposal. Here are some tips to make each of these three encounters as positive an experience as possible for even the most critical reviewer.

The First Impression: Initial Scan Encounter

Think like a reviewer for a minute and imagine what would make a proposal attractive to you. First, you would like to see a proposal that is thin and therefore can be reviewed quickly rather than a thick and ponderous tome. This means *limit the appended material to the absolute essentials,* such as letters of commitment and one- to two-page résumés of key personnel. A lot of novice applicants think that the reviewer will be favorably impressed by thick and weighty proposals (implying complex and thoughtfully developed projects), but in fact just the opposite is true. Given that most appended material does not bear directly on the selection criteria, most reviewers will spend little or no time reading it. Their time is an extremely precious commodity that is better spent reading the narrative and rating the proposals against the selection criteria.

You can also enhance your proposal's first impression by *organizing the narrative according to the required elements* rather than according to a different set of headings that you think make more sense than the selection criteria. That means making your major headings the same as the selection criteria, and minor headings the same as any subheadings within the selection criteria. When the reviewers can quickly and efficiently find the narrative associated with each of the selection criteria, they can happily proceed without the frustration generated by a proposal format that bears little resemblance to the selection criteria.

Finally, you can greatly improve your proposal's first impression by *making the narrative appear to be an easy read.* For example, a reviewer will be grateful to see lots of white space on each page (double-spacing, generous margins), a 12-point or larger font, and ample use of tables and charts, which are easier to read late at night and break up the monotony of endless pages of narrative.

The Second Impression: Reading and Rating Encounter

Again, think like a reviewer. If you were looking at a proposal, what would most impress you as you started to read it? Probably a proposal that reads as if it was written just for you! How can the applicant do that? One strategy is to *find out what kinds of reviewers are going to be looking at the proposals so you can tailor your writing accordingly.* Are they predominantly university researchers or teachers in schools, for example? The answer to that question could tell you a lot about how to write your proposal so that it appears to be tailored to the kinds of people who are doing the review. You can find out who the potential peer reviewers are by contacting the project officer identified in the RFP for your grant competition.

Another "second impression" strategy is to *highlight (boldface, italicize) key words from the selection criteria* as they appear in your proposal. By doing so, you guide reviewers to the most important narrative in your proposal as they look to match your words to their selection criteria. Also, identify key terms in the selection criteria and use the same terms in your narrative. If you have questions about the interpretations of key words and concepts, contact the project officer as you write your proposal and clarify how the reviewers will apply these concepts.

Finally, to make the most favorable second impression and to maximize the number of points each section earns, *align the number of pages you write about each element to the proportion of total possible points associated with that element.* For example, if the "Quality of Project Design" criterion accounts for 25 of a possible 100 points and the maximum number of pages of narrative is 40, your narrative on this section should be about 10 pages in length. Straying too much from this point allocation/page allocation formula indicates a mismatch between what you think is important and what the reviewer is required to weigh as important.

The Third Impression: Panel Review Encounter

To make the best possible third impression—the one in which you make the most critical reviewer your ally in the panel discussion/review process—we suggest two strategies.

First, *present a compelling or creative idea for your project,* one that makes it hard for even the most critical reviewer not to recognize its value. In some cases you may not be offering a completely new idea or design, but you should make the case convincingly and enthusiastically that it is the right project at the right time in the right place.

Second, *paginate every single page of the proposal in sequence, including the appended material,* even if you have to write the page numbers by hand. This may seem like an insignificant matter, but nothing is more irritating to a reviewer who wants to discuss a section of your proposal in the panel review than not having a page number to refer to.

Variations to the Federal Grant Application Review Process

We have walked you through an extensive, thorough, and multistage review process—that of the federal demonstration grant—to help you understand the process from a reviewer's perspective and be a more effective grant writer. However, many review processes are somewhat different from the federal process; they are often not as detailed or extensive. For example, a typical review process for a private foundation may start with the submission of an initial letter of intent—a brief presentation of your project concept and your qualifications to carry it out. This letter may be reviewed by a project officer and a review panel who will then ask you for a full proposal if they like the concept. You submit the proposal according to the specified guidelines, and by the deadline, for a final decision. Grants officers, as front-line screeners of incoming proposals, may develop recommendations for a board of trustees or similar decision-making group regarding final awards. Regardless of the differences in review processes, your proposal must make a good impression every step of the way.

Many grant review processes at corporate foundations follow a similar pattern. Some grants processes at private and corporate foundations are even simpler and eliminate the step of submitting an initial letter or preliminary proposal. The simpler processes also generally correlate with smaller average grant awards. And some foundation RFPs are structured as a series of questions for the applicant to respond to. This format lends itself well to proposals submitted electronically via the corporation's or foundation's Web site. A good example is available at http://www.verizon.com/.

Regardless of what sort of review process your proposal is subjected to, the better the impression it makes, the more likely it will be funded.

A Reminder About Relationships

The grants officer is an important part of the peer review process. The grants officer serves as the liaison between the grant applicant and the final decision-making panel. Therefore, your relationship with the grants officer may be significant to the final decision about your grant application. It is important to know your audience and to write your proposal with the audience's (customer's) interests in mind. The grants officer can become an advocate for your project or a barrier to its continued consideration for funding. Take the time to develop a rapport with the grants officer and address her concerns and recommendations.

The Value of Becoming a Grant Reviewer

From a grant-writing perspective, serving as a reviewer provides tremendous insights that can inform your own applications. The experience will greatly enhance your understanding of the process, people, and priorities of the funder, making you a much smarter potential applicant. Rebecca served as a reviewer for the 2001 Dropout Prevention Demonstration grant competition and for the 2000 Smaller Learning Communities Grant competition, both through the U.S. Department of Education (US DOE). Subsequently, she was a technical writer for three successful grant applications (the 21st Century Commu-

nity Learning Centers demonstration grant competition—US DOE; the Elementary School Counselor demonstration grant competition—US DOE; and an Eisenhower Professional Development grant, VT DOE). Rich served for a year as a PEP Net Awards reviewer in 1999, before applying the next year on behalf of his own organization. The application and review process is rigorous and competitive. The insights Rich gained by participating in the review process helped his organization become one of only seven new organizations receiving PEP Net recognition nationally in 2000.

You don't need to pass a high-stakes test to be a grant reviewer. If you are qualified, interested, and available, your services can be put to good use as a peer reviewer. Because federal demonstration grants can sometimes prove to be overly bureaucratic, consider becoming a reviewer for state-level grants. Contact your state department of education, health and human services agency, or department of justice or labor about this possibility. The Web sites for these agencies will often identify recently awarded competitive grants for specific programs and include the name, phone number, and e-mail address of a grants officer. These people are great starting points for inquiring about reviewing grants within their agency. Try to identify grant programs that align with your own professional experience and interests to demonstrate that you would be a qualified reviewer. If you want to become a reviewer for a federal demonstration grant, contact the grants officer in charge of the competition and inquire about the possibility.

Private and corporate foundations don't normally seek outside reviewers, but in some circumstances, such as starting up a new program outside their usual areas of grant making, they may seek experts from the field. You can inquire directly to a grants officer or grant program director, who is often identified on the foundation Web site.

KEY POINTS TO REMEMBER

❑ Your proposal needs to make a positive first impression and a positive lasting impression.

❑ Find out what kinds of reviewers are going to be looking at the proposals.

❑ Limit your proposal appendices to the absolute essentials.

❑ Make the proposal narrative appear to be an easy read by organizing it according to the selection criteria and highlighting key terms from the selection criteria.

❑ Align the number of pages you write about each selection criterion to the proportion of total possible points associated with that criterion.

❑ Present compelling and creative project ideas that inspire reviewers.

❑ Number each page of the proposal consecutively, including the appendices.

❑ Establish a relationship with a grants officer who can play a critical role in the review process.

❑ Consider becoming a grant reviewer to become a much smarter grant applicant.

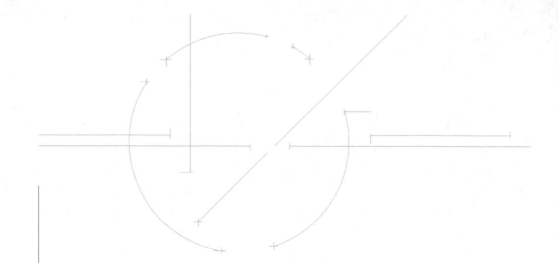

5

After "The Call"

Congratulations! Not only have you made it through the arduous task of convening groups of stakeholders to complete the RFP process—you have written a winning proposal! The funding source has recognized the potential in what you plan to do; your project mission, values, and priorities are compelling; and your plan for implementation, management, and evaluation is strong. Take the time to enjoy the euphoria that often accompanies this financial affirmation and acknowledgment of your hard work—it is important to celebrate achievements in life. Hang up the phone, put down the letter, and share the good news with your colleagues; trade high-fives before the reality of what lies ahead truly sets in. You have the money to support your program. Now what do you do?

You shouldn't assume that because your project was funded it will be successful. What looked good on the menu doesn't necessarily taste good when you eat it. Managing and sustaining your project is a challenge, but the straightforward strategies we provide can help catapult your project to success. The second half of this book focuses on what to do once you get the grant. Again, it isn't rocket science. It takes time and energy, but if your desired outcomes are truly important, the time and energy are well spent.

The Essentials of Weeks 1 Through 12

Sustainability is not something that you go out and get, nor is it something that just happens. Sustainability consists of the actions that you take to carry out your initiative extremely well, so that sustaining it just makes sense to the rest of the world (especially your partners and potential partners).

It is important to recognize that the skills required to successfully navigate the grant-writing process are vastly different from those necessary to effectively manage and implement a project. *Grant management is twice as hard as grant writing,* according to Donna Fernandez, who maintains the award-winning Web site *School Grants* (http://www.schoolgrants.org) and has raised $6 million in grant funding since 2001 for a nonprofit organization that supports charter schools for students at risk (Allen, 2003).

In the same way that getting a grant resembles getting a job, launching and sustaining your project can be compared with starting a new job—say, again, a teaching position. You've gone through the extensive application and review process, and the school district has selected you for the position. If the job appears to be a good match and the school district intends to make good use of your strengths and abilities, you are probably excited. But soon the thrill will subside, and you'll be faced with pressing administrative issues (such as getting your W2s and insurance forms completed, moving into your office space, and ordering textbooks). Once you're in the classroom, you will need to identify and connect with your colleagues around the building and the district. If you want your

job for the long term, you'll need to effectively carry out your professional responsibilities, which include working with others, teaching, developing goals, increasing student learning outcomes, and assessing progress toward achievement.

Now think about this. The grant funder has seen the value in your ideas and wants to financially support your project. All the hard work in the grant-writing process paid off, and it feels good. Now, as the grantee, you must complete and submit multiple forms, paperwork, and documentation. You need to find and secure physical space in which to operate your project and house personnel. You are responsible for implementing your project, which means you must think about collaborating with your partners, delivering quality services and activities, and evaluating project progress toward obtaining outcomes. To sustain the project activities and outcomes, you will need to communicate with your program partners regularly and engage in the ongoing assessment and evaluation of project activities and achievements.

Returning to the job analogy, once you get the job, you have to be good at what you do—at least as good as you appeared to be on your résumé and through the application process. Likewise, even a well-funded grant-sponsored project is unlikely to make a positive difference in the lives of others if it can't effectively implement and sustain what the initial proposal said it would.

Phase 1: Within Four Weeks of Notification

Once the notification excitement has subsided a bit, it's time to get moving. Here are some of the tasks that should be at the top of your to-do list.

Thank Your Project Officer and Ask About Next Steps

Regardless of how you received notice of your grant award, it is important to make an immediate personal connection with the funding agency and the individual identified as your official project officer. Call the appropriate people within two days of notification (including those persons from the funding organization with whom you had the most contact throughout the grant application and review process) to express your excitement about next steps. Remember, it's all about relationships.

In your conversation with your project officer or contact person, convey your commitment to carrying out the project with integrity and then ask what next steps you need to take to ensure the smooth allocation of funds from their organization to yours. Use this post-notification conversation to determine the forms you will be expected to fill out and to identify the materials you will need to provide to the funding agency. If the grant you have been funded for is being used to support any part of an existing program, you may have to provide the new funder with documentation of your pre-existing sources of funding.

Requested documentation varies tremendously, and many funders try to make sure they get what they need through the RFP process. State grantors tend to be particularly demanding in terms of supplemental documentation. They often want a complicated signed agreement; recent (and preferably audited) financial statements; a copy of the organization's liability coverage; a list of the board of directors; a signed form requesting initial payment; and assurance forms related to lobbying, drug-free workplace, and others. Some private and corporate foundations, on the other hand, send you a congratulatory letter, a check, and a simple request for annual progress reports. Read requests for documentation carefully, and clarify the process for requesting budget modifications and adjustments that may come up in the future.

Keep in mind that any mismanagement of the bureaucratic process at this point will delay or impede the transfer of grant funds, so you need to determine the information that will allow you to receive funds free and clear. Don't hesitate to ask questions. In fact, as long as it is not excessive, asking questions is another part of relationship building; it makes the project officer feel valued and trust that you really want to do it right. As we educators like so say, "there's no such thing as a bad question."

Negotiate the Budget with the Project Officer

Sometimes funders award a grant at a lower amount, perhaps considerably lower, than you requested in your grant application. This may happen for various reasons:

❑ Your proposed budget may have allocated money for materials, technology, or some other category of funding that appears to be too far removed from the participants and ultimate recipients of your program's services and activities.

❑ From the perspective of the funding agency, it appears that you can accomplish your overall program goals with less money than you anticipated.

❑ The original source of funding has been reduced, and therefore all projects funded by the source, including yours, must reduce their budgets across the board by some predetermined percentage.

❑ The funder may have determined that a number of projects were worth funding and decided to make smaller awards to more projects.

Whatever the reason, you will need to decide if you can accomplish your program goals with a reduced amount. Usually you can find a way to make it work, but not always. You may also be able to negotiate modifying your goals and expected outcomes in line with the reduced funding. Work collaboratively and diplomatically with your project officer to negotiate a budget that is mutually satisfying. Don't give in too easily, but be ready to compromise.

Some project directors prioritize changes based on what they think they can cover through other funding sources. If you are in doubt about the funder's willingness to cover particular costs, call and check with the grants officer. Try to keep administrative and operating expenses in the budget because these are the toughest to cover with other sources. Be sure to keep something in the project that matches the funder's priorities *and* that you know you can demonstrate results for. This increases the likelihood of continuing support.

Remember that your project officer may have little or no control over the amount allocated to your project. But, under the best of circumstances and relationships, the project officer can be a true ally and advocate.

Notify Your Partners

Once you have thanked the project officer, confirmed what you need to do to secure the allocation of grant funds to your organization, and negotiated a starting budget, share the good news with your partners. If someone other than you was identified in the RFP as the project director, be sure to contact that person first and confirm that he or she is still on board. Do the same with your organizational partners. Organizational partners include all those entities that have made a commitment to the project as outlined in the RFP in terms of time, resources, and personnel. Typically they include all the individuals whose letters of support you included in the grant application. Communicate with your key contact at each partnering agency, either by phone, e-mail, or in person, within one week of award notification. Follow up this one-on-one conversation with a letter or an e-mail that confirms the existence of the grant award and sets the stage for the series of meetings that will take place in Phase 2.

Publicize Your Award

Undoubtedly you believe that your program will make a real and sustained difference in the lives of others, and perhaps more important, an outside panel of reviewers selected your project out of many as being worthy of funding. So let the world know! The first step in getting the word out is to issue a press release such as the one shown in Figure 5.1. The Durant Independent School District in Oklahoma released a variation of this press release after receiving notification that its RFP was considered a winning proposal in the peer review process for the Safe Schools/Healthy Students Initiative and would be awarded $3 million. (Please note that some identifying information was deleted and some content condensed for clarity.)

No matter how large your grant award is, an effective press release includes the following universal elements:

❑ **For Immediate Release**—These words should appear in the upper left-hand margin, just under your letterhead. You should capitalize every letter.

❑ **Contact Information**—Skip a line or two after the release statement and list the name, title, e-mail address, telephone numbers, and fax number of your organization's spokesperson (the person with the most information). It is important to include a home telephone number because reporters often work on deadline and may not be available until after regular business hours.

❑ **Headline**—Skip two lines after your contact information and use boldface type. In a sentence or phrase, provide the headline that you want released.

❑ **Dateline**—This should be the school district and the town or city that your press release is issued from and the date you are mailing your release.

❑ **Lead Paragraph**—The first paragraph needs to grab the reader's attention and present basic information such as the "five Ws" (who, what, when, where, why). It should tell *who* is involved with the project, *what* project was funded and the amount of funding, *when* the project was funded and how long it will be funded, *where* the project will be based or what location it will serve, and *why* the project was funded.

5.1 Sample Press Release

FOR IMMEDIATE RELEASE
January 07, 2004

Media Contact: Delinda Knox
                580-920-4930
                dknox@durantisd.org

The Durant Public Schools announced today that the district and its community partners have been awarded a $3 million grant, funded over a three-year period, from the federal Safe Schools/Healthy Students Initiative (DOE, DOJ, DOHHS) to reduce violence and increase mental health services in Durant schools. "This grant has the potential to have more impact—academically, on school safety, and on the mental health of our students—than anything we've ever done before," said Duane Meredith, Assistant Superintendent. "Violence prevention and school safety are vital to providing our students with the tools and environment they need to succeed in the classroom and in life," said Greg Howse, Project Director. "The Safe Schools/Healthy Students grant helps us to implement programs and services to foster safe school environments and promote healthy youth development."

Building on the initiative's collaborative framework, Durant's Safe Schools/Healthy Students mission brings together students, parents, educators, mental health agencies, politicians, law enforcement, and faith organizations to talk about violence prevention. In turn, Durant and its partners will tailor their programs to address six elements:
1. Safe school environment
2. Violence, alcohol, and other drug prevention and early intervention
3. School and community mental health preventive and treatment intervention services
4. Early childhood psychosocial and emotional development
5. Truancy within our schools
6. School safety policies

LifeSkills® is a three-year intervention program initiated in the 6th grade and continued in the 7th and 8th grades as the students progress through the school system. The program is designed to prevent or reduce gateway drug use, i.e., tobacco, alcohol, and marijuana. In addition the students are provided with general self-management skills and social skills. Functional Family Therapy (FFT) is an empirically grounded, well-documented, and highly successful family intervention program for family and youth. It is designed to work with a wide range of at-risk youth aged 11–18 and their families, including youth with problems such as disruptive behavior, aggressive behavior, and substance abuse. Second Step®: A Violence Prevention Curriculum is a universal prevention program. It is taught to every student in the classroom rather than to selected children. The Second Step® curriculum encompasses preschool through middle school and is designed to promote social competence and reduce children's social and emotional problems. Character Counts® is a curricular framework based upon the six pillars: (1) trustworthiness, (2) respect, (3) responsibility, (4) fairness, (5) caring, and (6) citizenship. The Student Assistance Program is an identification and intervention process designed to assist students with issues interfering with learning, such as, but not limited to, emotional distress, family problems, or alcohol and other drug addiction.

The community is invited to a kick-off celebration, during which you will have an opportunity to find out about more of the exciting things the Safe Schools/Healthy Students Team has planned for Durant's schools. The event will be held on Monday, January 12, beginning at 4:00 p.m. at Durant High School.

Source: Retrieved from http://www.durantisd.org/safeschools/press.htm.

❑ **Text**—The main body of the press release is where your message should fully develop. Describe your project and the source of funding that supports it.

❑ **Recap**—At the lower-left-hand corner of the last page, restate the goals of the initiative, highlight an upcoming project event, and indicate where to go for further information.

Remember you are writing for the media, not for other education practitioners per se. You must tailor the language of your press release so that it captures your project clearly and in friendly, easy-to-understand language. You should also be aware of any specifications your funder may have about publicity related to their grants. Some corporate foundations, for example, will ask that you incorporate their logo and use specific wording regarding their award. If you're not sure, check with your grants officer.

In addition to your own press release, be sure to work with your partners to access their means of generating publicity. Encourage your partners to issue press releases and to publicize the project activities that the grant award will support.

Set Up Accounting Procedures

As soon as possible after receiving notification of your grant award, do what you need to do to establish the fiscal and administrative infrastructure of your project. Don't start from scratch if you don't have to. Most organizations, such as school districts and universities, have a system for accounting already in place that you can use (and will be expected to use) for your project accounting. If a bookkeeper is not available through the existing system to attend to the needs of your project, hire one as soon as possible. A project director needs to be sure that a system is in place for invoicing, cutting checks, and paying staff health benefits, for example. A project director will need a go-to person to determine how to request funds, get the bills paid, and ensure payment of benefits for staff members.

Phase 2: Within Eight Weeks of Notification

Once you've taken care of the basic activities of Phase 1, it's time to tackle some other high-priority concerns.

Determine an Appropriate Organizational Structure

Regardless of its size or scope, every project must have the capacity for effective management, budgeting, marketing, strategic planning, and evaluation. An appropriate organizational structure must exist to support each of these considerations. Do not skimp or overindulge in the establishment of an organizational structure. Configure it in a way that adequately reflects the scope and scale of your project.

For very small-scale projects, one person, perhaps the project director, can adequately address all of the short- and long-term administrative needs. Large-scale projects with an extensive scope may require at least one project director working with a management team, a board of directors or community advisory board, and an executive committee.

What Is a Management Team? The management team is the group of individuals that the project director works most closely with to make key operational decisions. This group meets with the project director fairly regularly, typically once a month, to discuss and make decisions related to the procurement and allocation of funds, adherence to policy, major programmatic midcourse corrections, and developing and executing agreements with partnering agencies.

What Is a Board of Directors or a Community Advisory Board? Nonprofit entities are legally required to have a board of directors that functions in an advisory and decision-making capacity. And most initiatives can benefit from regular input (quarterly, for example) from a diverse cross-section of individuals outside the regular management structure who share your programmatic vision and who will legally commit themselves to engage on behalf of the project and its ideals. A community advisory board provides similar guidance and direction but is not legally responsible for the work of the organization.

The goal is to put together a diverse group of people who are connected to the issues that your project addresses. Generally, the more clout, standing, skill, and influence they have in your community, the better off your project will be. For example, if your project is attempting to make curricular changes within the schools, seek out a professor or administrator from a local university's teacher preparation program. If your project is focused on adolescent literacy, seek out advisory board members through local library associations. Consider adding a local legislator to your advisory council. Members of the advisory group will have unique knowledge and connections. As one project director said, "You never know when that knowledge and those connections will pay off."

Here's a real-life example of how Rich, as a project director, strategically designed a board of directors. Linking Learning to Life (LLL) is a nonprofit regional initiative in northern Vermont that seeks to make connections between K–12 learning and the world of work. At the outset, Rich contacted the Lake Champlain Regional Chamber of Commerce, which already had a school-to-work council. He invited all members of this group to be part of the new LLL board of directors. He shared with them the goals and intended outcomes of LLL and asked if they would be interested in being on the board. In addition, he asked key representatives from business, higher education, youth and family services, and vocational rehabilitation to join the board. Those who expressed an interest were asked to describe why they wanted to be part of the board (to assess their level of commitment) and were brought together for a brainstorming session. At that session they determined what would be expected from board members in terms of time, resources, and financial (if any) commitments in addition to their legal responsibilities.

What Is an Executive Committee? Some projects require another layer of more frequent input and support for the project director than a management team and board can provide. This often takes the form of an executive committee, which is made up of a subgroup of individuals drawn from the management team, the board of directors, or the advisory board. This committee typically meets every other week to help guide the work.

Regardless of which organizational management structures you put in place, it is important to create a structure that will clearly benefit the project. Don't create structures just to look good on paper or just to hold meetings. Consider the scope of your project. Will it offer many different kinds of services and activities, or does it have a narrow focus? Does it serve a wide variety of participants or only a few? Consider the scale of your project. Is it receiving a great deal of funding or not so much? Will a few people be employed by the project or a large number? Will it serve many people across a wide region or a small number locally?

In general, the greater the scope and the larger the scale, the more complex and layered your organizational structure needs will be.

Once you choose your structure, establish a regular meeting schedule for each organizational group. Whip out those palm pilots and daytimers and schedule regular meetings. (A typical schedule is every two weeks for staff meetings, every two weeks for executive committee meetings, every month for management team meetings, and quarterly for advisory board meetings.) Everyone should commit to 100 percent attendance. Uniform and public recognition of the importance of these meetings is crucial at the onset of the grant. Regardless of the type of organizational structure you have, face-to-face communication must be consistent and ongoing. A sure sign that commitment to the project is strong is regular, on-time attendance at all meetings.

Reconvene Key Stakeholders for an All-Project Meeting

Discussion is considered to be one of the most powerful and effective strategies for promoting critical thought, encouraging reflective analysis, and generating a sense of collaboration. The group that gathers for this all-project meeting should include the project director and those teachers, administrators, curriculum coordinators, subcontractors, partnering agencies, and other key stakeholders with a vested interest in the project implementation. Be sure to notify people well ahead of time; the stakeholder meeting should be well attended. (Having refreshments never hurts!) The meeting of key stakeholders has three purposes:

❑ To celebrate the grant award and kick-start the project's collaborative energy

❑ To revisit the goals and objectives of the project

❑ To formulate a process for hiring project personnel

Celebrate the Grant Award and Kick-Start the Project's Collaborative Energy. As discussed in the introduction to this book, an increasing number of educational, business, and human services organizations consider collaboration to be a powerful strategy to achieve a vision and to address complex societal issues far more effectively than would be possible if they worked separately. In many respects, collaboration has become both the vehicle for obtaining student and school-level outcomes and a long-term outcome in itself. With that in mind, it is time to bring the people involved in the grant development process back to the table and get excited about what you can accomplish together. You'll want to reintroduce yourselves to each other, welcome new participants, and get ready to move forward. This meeting is about much more than planning logistics; it is about generating synergy and rekindling the enthusiasm you created during the grant-writing process.

To rekindle the enthusiasm, distribute the now-funded proposal as a fully bound copy in a nice three-ring notebook with an attractive cover. Personalize the notebook cover with the name of each stakeholder. Include a copy of your press release and a chart showing the organizational structure, including all staff member positions, the project management/operations team, executive committee, and board of directors or advisory board (as applicable). Include each person's name, title, primary responsibilities, location, and contact information. You will use the chart as a tool for discussion. Once everyone has the materials, flip through the grant together to become reacquainted with where things are in the proposal so they will be easy to reference during the discussion.

Sometimes the funding agency, particularly for large federal demonstration grants, sends various paraphernalia to winning applicants. From various grantors we've received T-shirts, coffee mugs, tote bags, hats, key chains, sticky-note pads, pins, and ballpoint pens, among other things. If your funder doesn't send you nifty items to distribute, consider creating something inexpensive on your own, such as pencils stamped with the name of your project or logo. Don't underestimate the power of this gesture with stakeholders. Everyone loves a token of appreciation, and it can trigger a sense of teamwork and pride.

Revisit the Goals and Objectives of the Project. Often a great deal of time—usually months, occasionally a year—passes between the submission of the grant application and the notice of acceptance and funding. It is crucial that the partners gather at the same table and familiarize themselves once again with the project's intended mission, activities, and outcomes. Often new personnel, such as a new director at a partnering community agency or a new principal, will have come on board during the time that the RFP application was under review; these individuals will need to be brought up to speed. If possible, have someone facilitate a discussion among stakeholders. Even if you don't have a trained facilitator, be sure that the meeting is being recorded or that someone is taking detailed notes. Use the following questions as a guide for the discussion:

❑ What are the desired outcomes of this program? What are the goals? What are we trying to accomplish within the next month? quarter? year(s)?

❑ How will we get there? What activities have we identified that will enable us to reach the project outcomes? What strategies are we using to reach our goals?

❑ Let's begin thinking about outcomes. What will indicate to us, and to the community, that we are making progress toward our desired short- and long-term outcomes?

Be sure to allocate enough time to have a thoughtful and thorough discussion and to address the issues at this initial project kick-off meeting with stakeholders. The time required depends upon the size of the group, the skills of the facilitator, the scope of the initiative, and the degree of collaboration and consensus developed to date. Typical stakeholder meetings of this nature take between two hours and a full day. Future meetings of the various organizational subgroups (staff, management team, executive committee, advisory board) will be much shorter.

Formulate a Process for Hiring Project Personnel. You've got the funds, so bring on the people! As most project directors will tell you, it is imperative that you take the time to hire the most appropriate and effective people to be part of your staff. When the Harvard Family Research Project posed the question "What is the single most important ingredient for creating, sustaining, and improving program quality?" to leaders in the field of child and family services, the overwhelming response was "high-quality and well-trained program staff" (Weiss, 2004). It is essential that you spend the time necessary to hire people that you and your partners feel good about. Use the organizational chart to verify the names and responsibilities of those who have already been hired or assigned to the project. Determine the positions that still need to be filled and the primary organization responsible for hiring for that position. If a project director is not yet on board, hire one as soon as possible. Often an individual who is involved in the grant-writing process has made a commitment to direct the project if it is awarded funding, and time needn't be spent looking for and hiring a director. However, the intended project director identified in the proposal may not be available to assume this role by the time the project is funded. In that case, a new project director should be selected and endorsed collaboratively by the project partners. Project leaders should seek to hire someone who values the goals of the project and has the requisite skills and attributes to make the project a success.

A word about grant writers as project directors: *Grant writers don't necessarily make the best project directors*. The skills and abilities necessary to craft a winning grant proposal are unique and essential, but they are not the same as those necessary to lead and manage a project. Primary grant writers should be considered for the position of project director only if they have all the necessary prerequisite skills and abilities. Too often we have seen projects sink into confusion because of an inability to distinguish between the ability to develop and write a grant proposal and the ability to sustain a vision, supervise staff, and build long-term organizational capacity.

Meet with project partners to form a hiring subcommittee to carry out the advertising, interviewing, and hiring process for each open position. You'll want to work cooperatively to craft the actual job descriptions, submit them to the appropriate advertising outlets, set interview schedules, and conduct the interviews. The project director or at least one key project leader should help formulate the job descriptions, ensuring that job responsibilities and professional prerequisites as defined make sense given the overall objectives of the project, and that each job is strategically aligned so that roles and responsibilities do not overlap or conflict with one another.

Make sure to take the time in recruitment and screening of potential employees to ensure you have the right people for the jobs to be done. Do what you need to do to clearly define job responsibilities, advertise, and interview potential staff. Hiring the wrong people may have irreparable long-term consequences for the project. Use as many traditional media outlets as possible (while staying within your organizational budget) to get the word out about job opportunities. Don't rely on word-of-mouth or people you know. Access the Internet, newspapers, agency networks, and professional listservers.

Once new staff are hired, get them into the system as soon as possible. Most personnel coming into school districts for the first time will need to complete and file a number of documents, including federal and state tax reporting forms, drug-free workplace verification, benefits questionnaires, and security information, including a fingerprint check.

Develop a Media Plan. Regardless of how simple or complex, broad or finely targeted your overall project activities and services might be, the media—including the press, television, radio, and the Internet—can help you achieve them. Whether you want to publicize a new community service established through your grant or highlight how your program is helping individuals in your community, the media are a valuable tool. The media are also useful when a national issue affects your community or if a situation occurs locally that involves stakeholders affected by your project. By forming a strong partnership with your local media, you will enhance goodwill and positive public perception for your project, which enhances long-term community support. You can use the spreadsheet in Figure 5.2 to begin locating and recording informa-

5.2 Media Outlet Contact Information

Newspapers/ Print Media	How often published?	Key Contact Person, Phone Number, E-mail Address, Fax Number, and Mailing Address		
		Education/Youth Issues	Community Events	Other _____
Television Programs	Which station? How often aired?	Key Contact Person, Phone Number, E-mail Address, Fax Number, and Mailing Address		
		Education/Youth Issues	Community Events	Other _____
Radio Programs	Which station? How often aired?	Key Contact Person, Phone Number, E-mail Address, Fax Number, and Mailing Address		
		Education/Youth Issues	Community Events	Other _____
Web Sites	How often updated?	Key Contact Person, Phone Number, E-mail Address, Fax Number, and Mailing Address		
		Education/Youth Issues	Community Events	Other _____

tion about appropriate media outlets, including frequency of publication or broadcast and contact information for key staff members associated with various issues. Update this form regularly and refer to it often.

Phase 3: Within 12 Weeks of Notification

In addition to the various activities in Phases 1 and 2, a few more tasks need your attention to ensure that your project stands on a firm, future-oriented foundation.

Determine the Need for and Secure Physical Space, Furniture, and Equipment

Beyond getting the appropriate personnel on board, it is important to secure physical work space for them. If you are hiring many new people from outside your home organization (outside the school district, for example) and the initiative is comprehensive in scope and sequence, it might be necessary to have one centralized location as a home base. The Poudre School District in Fort Collins, Colorado, as the recipient of a $5.6 million, three-year grant for a Safe Schools/Healthy Students Initiative (for which Rebecca was the evaluator), acquired a building and a small piece of property to house Project LINK. This office space was used by the project director, the assistant to the director, five mental health clinicians, and four curriculum specialists—most of

whom were hired from outside of the school district.

Securing a large structure for office space may not always be feasible or necessary, but be sure that all staff members have a place to do their paper and computer work, receive and make telephone calls, and access e-mail and the Internet. Many 21st Century Community Learning Center initiatives are able to secure physical space, furniture, and equipment from within existing school settings and don't need additional outside space or technology. In either case, leave no stone unturned. Be sure to provide for adequate telephone, copy machine, fax, storage, and meeting-space capabilities. Nothing causes early disgruntlement among staff more than not being able to carry out basic job functions because of insufficient space or inadequate equipment. And the closer together you can cluster staff, the more efficient their work together will be.

Negotiate Formal Agreements with Partnering Agencies and Organizations

Goodwill and the best intentions are great, but common sense suggests—and the law might require—that you secure formal contractual arrangements with each partnering agency that is a subcontractor on the grant. Meet with representatives of each partnering agency to revisit the roles and responsibilities that it has in achieving the outcomes of the funded project. The conversation should focus on the specific services and activities that the subcontractor will provide.

Out of this conversation will come the language that you will include in the formal memorandum of understanding (MOU) or letter of agreement (LOA) between the project lead agency and each partnering agency. The contract should be simple and concise. Usually the entity that is legally responsible for the grant funds (typically the local education agency or nonprofit organization) will use its predetermined format for an MOU or an LOA. If your organization does not have an MOU/LOA format you can use, you can draft your own using a template such as the one provided in Figure 5.3. Any MOU/LOA should include the following elements:

❏ Who is entering into a binding legal contract with whom
❏ What services or activities will be provided and how often
❏ The financial amount of the subcontract
❏ The duration of the contract
❏ Conditions for changing the contract
❏ Signature lines for those who have the authority to secure the contract
❏ Date lines

Once you have drafted an LOA or MOU, send it to the partnering agency for review and modification. Secure signatures on final copies and distribute to the appropriate entities.

5.3 Template for Memorandum of Understanding/Letter of Agreement

---

MEMORANDUM OF UNDERSTANDING/LETTER OF AGREEMENT

Between
[Name of Local Educational Authority/Organization here]
and
[Name of Partner Organization here]

This agreement articulates the roles and responsibilities of each named partner in implementing the [name of grant-funded program], funded by [name of funding source].

[Lead agency] agrees to the following:
[Identify roles and responsibilities here in bulleted or paragraph format.]
[Specify activities and services to be provided by local educational authority or organization.]

[Partner organization] agrees to the following:
[Identify roles and responsibilities here in bulleted or paragraph format.]
[Specify activities and services to be provided by partner agency.]

Financial conditions of the contract:
[Identify amount of subcontract to be awarded, if any, to partner agency.]
[Specify time frame and a process for proper allocation of funds.]

Duration of the contract:
[Specify the time period for which the agreement exists.]

Conditions for modifying the memorandum of understanding/agreement:
[Describe the process for making changes to the mutual agreement.]

WE, THE UNDERSIGNED, AGREE TO ADHERE TO THE AGREEMENT DESCRIBED ABOVE AND TO FULLY COLLABORATE TO ENSURE THE SUCCESSFUL IMPLEMENTATION OF THIS PROJECT.

_____   _____
Signature Line—Local Educational Authority   Date
Authorized Representative

_____   _____
Signature Line—Partner Agency   Date
Authorized Representative

WITHIN 4 WEEKS HAVE YOU . . .

❑ Thanked your project officer?

❑ Determined next steps and required documentation?

❑ Notified your partners?

❑ Publicized your award?

❑ Set up accounting and bookkeeping procedures?

WITHIN 8 WEEKS HAVE YOU . . .

❑ Determined an organizational structure for the project?

❑ Reconvened key stakeholders to
    - Kick-start collaborative energy?
    - Revisit goals and activities?

WITHIN 12 WEEKS HAVE YOU . . .

❑ Secured physical space, furniture, and equipment for staff?

❑ Staffed your initiative?

❑ Negotiated formal agreements with partnering agencies?

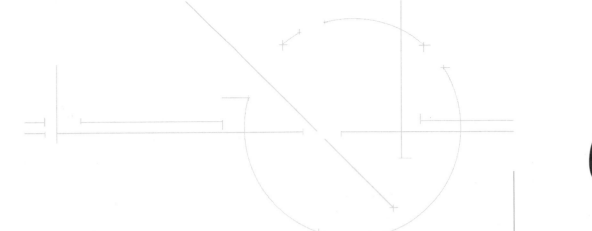

6

Program Evaluation: Prove What You Know

Each year billions of public and private dollars fund education initiatives, such as yours, that are designed to make a difference in the lives of children, families, and communities. Practitioners concerned with the delivery of grant-sponsored initiatives devote endless hours to project management but may have no idea how to tackle the often maligned task of evaluation. Compared with grant proposal writing and project implementation, program evaluation can seem daunting (and maybe even a waste of precious time, energy, and other resources). And yet, you'll inevitably find yourself asking, How are things going? Are we making a difference? Are the participants benefiting? How can we demonstrate that this program should be re-funded? What should be sustained and why? Can we show the funder that the investment was worthwhile? Given all the hard work that went into the proposal development and project planning, your initiative may be very successful, but you won't be able to recognize that success or sustain it over the long term unless you engage in effective evaluation.

In this chapter we demystify common evaluation terminology and present a series of strategies to simplify effective evaluation. Keep in mind that evaluation is your opportunity to showcase what your project is all about and the achievements that are important to you. It is quite likely, depending on your values and experience, that the evaluation you undertake after notification of your grant award will vary slightly (or significantly) from the one you outlined in the application and proposal development process.

This is not unusual. Your plan for just about everything outlined in your proposal (budget, activities, management, dissemination, evaluation) tends to shift after award notification. What's important is to clarify your evaluation plan as soon as possible.

Most grantors don't require, expect, want, or need complicated program evaluation; they want honest information about project achievements. In our experience, educators and social service practitioners have all the knowledge and skills necessary to engage in high-quality program evaluation. This chapter is intended to help you hone your natural skills in assessment and reflection and apply them to the evaluation of your initiative.

A thoughtful and thorough program evaluation cultivates project sustainability and typically involves six stages of emphasis, which are shown in Figure 6.1. Let's look at each of these stages in detail.

6.1 A General Framework for Project Evaluation

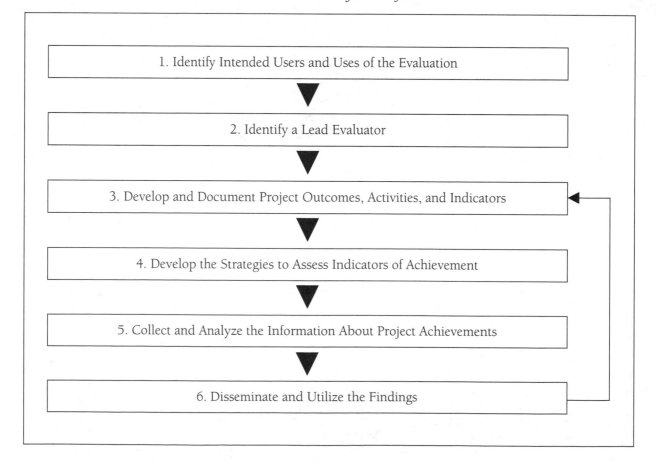

1. Identify Intended Users and Uses of the Evaluation

2. Identify a Lead Evaluator

3. Develop and Document Project Outcomes, Activities, and Indicators

4. Develop the Strategies to Assess Indicators of Achievement

5. Collect and Analyze the Information About Project Achievements

6. Disseminate and Utilize the Findings

1. Identify Intended Users and Uses of the Evaluation

Before taking a ride on the evaluation train, think about who your fellow passengers will be and where you are headed. Will there be lots of passengers and many stops along the way, or just a conductor and one ultimate destination? Ask yourself, Who will use the evaluation and for what purposes? It is important that you answer this question early on and as clearly as possible.

Program evaluation findings are generally used for some combination of the following three purposes: (1) to improve and develop the quality of project implementation (often referred to as *formative evaluation*), (2) to make judgments about project value and worth related to decisions about funding (also known as *summative evaluation*), and (3) to generate knowledge that can influence thinking about project-related issues in a more abstract way (sometimes called *conceptual evaluation* [Patton, 1997]). At a minimum, most of us want some degree of reliable information gathering and analysis that sheds light on the quality and quantity of our program's achievements so that we can adjust and improve what we do. Grant-sponsored initiatives like yours will likely need the information that an organized evaluation provides in order to respond to required performance reports or to showcase the achievement of outcomes as you make the case for increased or continued funding. Or you may want an evaluation to reveal information that can be used to inform a larger policy debate taking place locally, statewide, or nationally. Most program evaluations are a combination of all three types.

Here's a real-world example of a program evaluation and how it has been used. Rebecca was the lead evaluator for Peoples' Academy: Career Academy of the Arts (PACAA), which is a grant-sponsored secondary school initiative that provides a school-within-a-school experience for underengaged senior high school students with an affinity for the arts. PACAA's program evaluation included interviews with students and teachers to gather information about the quality of the curriculum. This information is being used to improve the delivery of the courses (formative evaluation). Another element of PACAA's program evaluation plan was the gathering of quantitative survey data that shed light on how the program affected student motivation and achievement. This information is being integrated into annual reports to grantors in order to showcase the achievement of outcomes and to make the case for continued funding (summative evaluation). Finally, the program evaluation examines how PACAA and its outcomes are related to principles of high school renewal, and these findings are being used by state task forces and policymakers (conceptual evaluation).

Typically, users of program evaluation vary widely, and you shouldn't assume that only funders want and need the information and insight that a well-planned evaluation can provide. A wide range of individuals including, but not limited to, project staff, teachers, directors, board members, project officers, potential funders, legislators, community members, tax payers, state task force members, and local administrators may have a vested interest in evaluation findings. However, you need to ascertain who the *primary* intended users will be. Remember that it is people, not organizations, who use evaluation findings. It is important to identify, by name, the primary individuals who will use the findings and to determine their purposes for such use. The worksheet in Figure 6.2 can help you identify and distinguish intended users and uses of your project evaluation.

2. Identify a Lead Evaluator

Someone must be responsible for leading the project's evaluation efforts. This could be someone from within the organization or from the outside. You'll need to think about the following factors:

- ❏ *The intended users of the evaluation:* Do they have a preference for who collects, analyzes, and reports the information?
- ❏ *The type of information you want to collect:* Is it a highly complex mix of statistical and narrative data or a relatively simple combination of numbers and words?
- ❏ *The data collection tools and methods to be used in the evaluation:* Do they already exist within your own organization or do they need to be created and developed?
- ❏ *The evaluation capacity of your organization:* Do project personnel have the abilities necessary to carry out quantitative and qualitative data collection methods and analyses?
- ❏ *The degree to which your project personnel recognize the worth and merit of evaluation:* Have project leaders and staff initiated and engaged in organizational evaluation and

6.2 Worksheet: Intended Uses and Intended Users for Project Evaluation

	Who will use the evaluation and for what purposes?	**Intended Users**			
		Project Management	Project Funders	Superintendent	Other ____
Intended Uses	*Formative:* To improve and develop the project				
	Summative: To make value judgments about the project				
	Conceptual: To influence thinking about project-related ideas				

assessment, or do they sidestep evaluation responsibilities?

❑ *The budgetary costs involved:* How much will it cost to use an external evaluator versus keeping evaluation activities and expenditures within the project?

❑ *Your level of access to qualified people:* Are there competent, trained, and experienced professionals within close proximity to your project headquarters?

External or Internal Lead Evaluator?

For a vast array of large-scale projects, the choice to use an external evaluator is probably a good one. When involved with the project from the beginning (ideally during the grant-writing process), a skilled evaluator can help facilitate the determination of intended use and intended users, help determine specific outcomes and measurable indicators, and help develop the most appropriate evaluation design. For an increasing number of federal grants, an external evaluator skilled in experimental and quasi-experimental research methods may be required to meet the absolute priorities of your grant. The RFP from the U.S. Department of Education's Office of Safe and Drug-Free Schools for their Partnerships in Character Education 2004 grants (previously referenced in Chapter 2) has an invitational priority for applications that propose experimental and quasi-experimental evaluation designs. They request the following:

projects under which participants—e.g., students, teachers, classrooms, or schools—are randomly assigned to participate in the project activities being evaluated or to a control group that does not participate in the project activities being evaluated. Evaluation plans that propose scientifically based research methods to assess the effectiveness of particular interventions . . . that determine whether the project produces meaningful effects on student achievement or teacher performance. When sufficient numbers of participants are available to support evaluation strategies that use experimental designs with random assignment or quasi-experimental designs using a match comparison group or regression continuity designs, applicants are encouraged to use one of these designs. The proposed evaluation plan should describe how the project evaluator will collect—before the project intervention commences and after it ends—valid and reliable data that measure the impact of participation in the program or in the comparison group. (http://www.ed.gov/legislation/FedRegister/announcements/2004-1/022404e.pdf)

Education and social service practitioners (and almost anyone else) will likely be intimidated or confused by this language and these requirements. Most of us aren't in the business of conducting systematic experimental designs. So in many cases, particularly for large federal grants, it may be essential to hire a highly skilled independent evaluator with the technical expertise needed to carry out evaluation plans of this nature.

Even for small-scale projects, some grant funders (and the tax-paying public) perceive project evaluation findings, conclusions, and analyses to be more valid when they are reported by individuals who are not involved with the implementation of the project. The assumption is that these individuals are more objective than internal staff closely affiliated with the delivery of services and activities.

Many factors should be taken into consideration when deciding who your lead evaluator will be. If you want help finding an independent evaluator, contact the American Evaluation Association at http://www.eval.org/. They provide a list of evaluation consultants at no charge. You can also contact the department at your local college or university that focuses on issues related to your project. For example, you could contact a university's department of education for help finding an evaluator for projects related to truancy, dropout prevention, literacy, school violence, or curriculum. Many universities (including Howard University, the University of Illinois at Urbana-Champaign, the University of Vermont) offer coursework, institutes, or a full graduate-degree program in evaluation; or they have evaluator consortiums made up of faculty and other personnel involved in all types of program evaluation. Land-grant institutions of higher education typically have an extension office that does a great deal of evaluation work with community organizations. They are also a good source for information about evaluation.

Most postsecondary institutions could provide guidance on whom to contact regarding your evaluation needs. And there are a whole host of independent evaluation consultants to be found through the yellow pages.

But don't let those federal calls for experimental designs scare you. We repeat: *Most grantors don't expect or want huge, complicated program evaluation.* Program evaluation is as much common sense as it is skill. And educators already bring essential evaluation-related skills to the table, including the ability to identify appropriate learning outcomes, generate assessments, analyze assessment information, and engage in reflective practice. Again, if you are willing and able to put in the time, you can do this!

3. Develop and Document Project Outcomes, Activities, and Indicators

The project outcomes, activities, and indicators that you articulated in your original grant proposal represented the best thinking of you and your partners at the time. It is true that initial development of your project's desired outcomes, activities, and indicators should take place during the planning stages of your project, ideally during the grant-writing process. However, once you receive your grant award—and then again on a regular basis (at least annually)—it is important to revisit your stated outcomes, activities, and indicators to ensure that they are focused and pragmatic and that they provide a current road map for your project that can be used for program evaluation purposes. Effective program evaluation requires that you have a clear picture of your project's outcomes, activities, and indicators. *Think of the outcomes as how you ultimately want participants to be affected by the project, the activities as what your project actually does and provides, and the indicators as the degree to which the project is carrying out its activities and making progress toward its outcomes.*

Outcomes are clearly defined, anticipated, and desired short- and long-term project effects. Outcomes focus on the realization of measurable or observable participant benefits and systems achievements. They are not pie-in-the-sky, overly idealistic, unattainable things that you can only hope your project will achieve. Project outcomes will provide the focus for *all* program evaluation activities, and each of the outcomes that you choose to identify will need to be measured or observed in some way. Outcomes should focus on what can realistically be accomplished during the period of program funding. Don't set your project up for failure. Because most grant funding is allocated for periods of less than three years, it rarely extends long enough to cover periods in which more long-term participant outcomes are likely to be realized.

Project *activities* are the services that your project provides to serve participants, to deliver training, or to create materials that you believe will ultimately lead to the achievement of short- and long-term outcomes. Project activities typically provide some type of direct service or information to participants, but their content and focus are diverse and far-reaching. There is no end to the types of activities that practitioners engage in to bring about desired outcomes.

Indicators act as the gauge to whether, and to what degree, your project is carrying out its activities and is making progress toward its outcomes. Indicators can be quantitative and qualitative in nature, which means that they can be represented by numbers and statistics, and by words and narratives.

Your lead evaluator and a few key people responsible for project evaluation should consider the following questions to develop realistic outcomes, key activities, and specific indicators of achievement:

❏ What are the *desired outcomes* of this program? What benefits do we hope and expect participants to experience in the short and long term? What effects will our project have?

❏ What *activities* will enable us to reach our outcomes? What direct services or information is the project providing to participants?

❏ What will *indicate* to us that we are making progress toward implementing our activities and attaining the desired outcomes? How will we gauge the extent to which we are delivering our activities and that these activities result in the achievement of outcomes?

Let's look at an example in practice. These discussion prompts were used to determine outcomes, activities, and indicators by the stakeholders involved in the Early Childhood Education Cares (ECE Cares) initiative funded through a U.S. Department of Education demonstration grant. The grant supports delivery of training and professional development to early childhood education teachers. The lead evaluator and a few other project personnel got together to share ideas about the ECE Cares program. They identified two primary users of the evaluation (the project director and the federal project officer) and three central uses (program development,

program marketing, and showcasing project worth in funding requests). Ultimately the discussion gave them the opportunity to document several essential outcomes, supporting activities, and corresponding indicators in the format found in Figure 6.3. Notice that indicators of success have been developed for a primary outcome of the project (increasing pro-social behavior, which is a summative indicator) *and* for a primary project activity (effective curriculum training, which is for formative evaluation purposes). However, the ECE Cares project determined indicators for several outcomes and multiple activities using this format. You should develop specific and realistic indicators for each of your central outcomes and major project activities.

6.3 Outcome, Activity, and Indicators for ECE Cares Project

Project Outcome 1	To increase the pro-social behavior of young children in early childhood settings throughout the community.
	Indicators
	a) Children in early childhood classroom settings will demonstrate an increase in pro-social behavior.
	b) Classroom climate survey results will show a positive increase in sense of well-being, safety, and belonging for students, staff, and families.
Project Activity 1	To offer effective ECE Cares skill curriculum training and professional mentoring to early childhood providers from public and nonpublic settings.
	Indicators
	a) Fifty early childhood education providers, from public and nonpublic settings, will be trained in the ECE Cares curriculum by the end of the first year.
	b) Participants will report that the ECE Cares training was delivered effectively and enhanced their teaching ability.

Additional Considerations

When you are developing and documenting your outcomes, activities, and indicators, be sure to keep in mind what may already be expected of or available to you. You should reread the RFP and other relevant documents from the funding agency to determine the highest-priority outcomes. Determine project outcomes that align with the "absolute priorities" of the funding source. A mismatch between the desired outcomes you have for your project and your funder's intentions may strain the relationship with the program officer and could jeopardize continued funding.

If possible, ascertain which indicators of effectiveness are already used by your school district and other organizations and determine if it makes sense for your project to use the same or similar indicators. For instance, your local school district may already keep track of attendance or GPA data that you could access and use as indicators of achievement for your project's outcomes.

The outcomes, activities, and indicators that are developed must be shared with all appropriate program personnel as soon as possible. It is essential that project staff know where the program is headed and how they will know if things are moving in the right direction. They need to be cued in to how they might be a part of the evaluation process and the role they play in delivering activities and reaching outcomes.

4. Develop the Strategies to Assess Indicators of Achievement

Understand the difference between quantitative and qualitative indicators of achievement. As we stated at the outset, indicators can be *quantitative* or *qualitative* in nature. From the ECE Cares example in Figure 6.3 we can see that the project personnel intend to assess numerical and narrative indicators. Typically, quantitative measures use numbers to describe indicators of program activities and outcomes. Quantitative measures may examine how many people are being served and how often (activity-related indicators); they may also examine changes in rates of achievement, such as academic test scores and high school completion (outcome-related indicators).

Qualitative indicators are usually gathered and reported through the use of narrative information or data represented by words and the perspectives of participants. Mechanisms for gathering narrative information include individual or focus group interviews, open-ended survey questions, and written observations of an activity in action. The perspectives of program participants, project staff, and other stakeholders are often captured through interviews, questionnaires, and observations conducted by a program evaluator.

As is the case with most grant-funded projects, quantitative and qualitative indicators are important to ECE Cares. They want to numerically assess how many providers they train (quantitative), document through narrative interview transcripts and Likert-scale surveys the personal perspectives of early childhood providers regarding enhancements in their teaching ability (qualitative and quantitative), and assess through daily record sheets and climate surveys the long-term effect of ECE Cares training in the classroom (quantitative).

It is important to determine as early as possible in the evaluation process both the strategies that will be used to assess and collect information about indicators of achievement and the individuals who will be responsible for collecting the project data. Once identified, the tools and the people responsible for using them can be inserted into a spreadsheet similar to the one shown in Figure 6.4. As the figure illustrates, the ECE Cares project determined and then documented quantitative and qualitative indicators, corresponding data collection tools and methods, and the persons responsible.

Common Data Collection Tools, Methods, and Strategies

Some of the evaluation methods used by the ECE Cares project are typical in program evaluation work. You may want to modify them for your project. These include (1) a Delivery of Services—Tracking and Update Form, (2) Likert-scale surveys, and (3) interview protocols.

Delivery of Services—Tracking and Update Form. To collect and record the quantitative information about the ECE Cares curriculum training, ECE Cares staff filled out a data collection form monthly. It was important for ECE Cares project personnel to document that participants in the ECE Cares training came from both public and private child care settings. In addition, they wanted to record the number of children in classroom settings with people trained in the ECE Cares curriculum. The ECE Cares trainer used a form similar to the Monthly Training Update Form shown in Figure 6.5 to log information on attendance at training sessions and to report project activity information. If your project needs to log certain program activities on an ongoing basis, you may want to modify this form for your own use; simply relabel the column headings to reflect the measures that you want to record and report.

Likert-Scale Surveys. Along with tracking and update forms, surveys are common means for collecting quantitative data about project indicators. Mechanisms for gathering survey information about a program's quality include close-ended questions, such as those that ask participants to rate their level of satisfaction with the services and information provided. More powerful evidence is often generated when survey participants are asked to rate the degree to which they have gained new skills or information, or changed their behavior as a result of their involvement in the

6.4 Outcome, Activity, Indicators, Tools, and Persons Responsible for ECE Cares Project

Project Outcome 1	To increase the pro-social behavior of young children in early childhood settings throughout the community.		
	Indicators	**Data Collection Tools/Methods**	**Person(s) Responsible**
	a) Children in early childhood classroom settings will demonstrate an increase in pro-social behavior.	Daily record sheets, indicating number and nature of verbal and physical interactions	School and community providers
	b) Classroom climate survey results will show a positive increase in sense of well-being, safety, and belonging for students, staff, and families.	Climate survey	Project evaluator
Project Activity 1	To offer effective ECE Cares skill curriculum training and professional mentoring to early childhood providers from public and nonpublic settings.		
	Indicators	**Data Collection Tool(s)**	**Person(s) Responsible**
	a) Fifty early childhood education providers, from public and nonpublic settings, will be trained in the ECE Cares curriculum by the end of the first year.	Monthly training update form	ECE Cares trainers
	b) Participants will report that the ECE Cares training was delivered effectively and enhanced their teaching ability.	Post-training Likert-scale survey	Project evaluator
		Follow-up focus group and individual interviews after training	Project evaluator

6.5 ECE Cares Monthly Training Update Form

Date	Number of service providers from the school district who completed ECE Cares training	Number of **service providers from private settings** who completed ECE Cares training	**Total number of service providers** who completed ECE Cares training	Total number of **children served** by providers trained in ECE Cares	Number of **service providers who have been observed on-site** after ECE Cares training
Aug. 2003	0	0	0	0	0
Sept. 2003	4	5	9	250	2
Oct. 2003	14	12	26	780	10
Current Totals	18	17	35	1,030	12

program. Likert scales, which attach values to a range of possible answers (such as Strongly Disagree, Strongly Agree, Never, Always) are commonly used to elicit numerical ratings from survey respondents in this manner.

The ECE Cares initiative used a written survey (Figure 6.6) of early childhood education providers to determine the extent to which the training helped practitioners improve their skills in relation to Outcome 1. This short survey provides a simple example of how to construct a Likert-scale instrument. You can expand and modify this type of survey to assess the specific activities of your particular project. Simply combine the scores of multiple participants and calculate an average response for each statement.

Interview Protocols. Interviews, either one-on-one or in a group forum often called a *focus group,* are a common method for obtaining qualitative information about the effects of project activities and outcomes. In general, choose to conduct individual interviews when you have fewer project participants and you want to understand effects in a deep way. Likewise, lean toward the use of focus groups when you have a greater number of project participants or participant groups or when you want to examine their perspectives in a broader (but by no means superficial) way. To develop an interview protocol, revisit your program's outcomes, indicators, and intended users. This will help you to refine and focus your interview questions so that you are sure to

6.6 Written Survey Format for ECE Cares Initiative

To what extent do you agree with the following statements? Please circle the box that most accurately reflects your response.

The ECE Cares training improved my ability to . . .

	5	4	3	2	1
. . . *model pro-social language for students.*	Strongly agree	Agree	Neither agree nor disagree	Disagree	Strongly disagree
. . . *structure the physical space for optimal student movement and access.*	Strongly agree	Agree	Neither agree nor disagree	Disagree	Strongly disagree
. . . *provide effective transitions from one classroom to the next.*	Strongly agree	Agree	Neither agree nor disagree	Disagree	Strongly disagree

capture the type of information you want and need. There are several questions that could be asked of staff and participants involved in almost any type of program to capture their perspectives on project effectiveness and value. The focus group and individual interview questions posed to ECE Cares staff and participants were similar to those provided in Figure 6.7.

Your project's particular outcomes, activities, and indicators will provide specific language that you can use to tailor your interview questions. Another possibility is to pose the questions as it appears in the figure, and then follow up with interview probes or prompts that elicit responses regarding the various components of the program. For

example, when asking about suggestions for improving the project, it is helpful to jog the interviewee's memory by listing specific program components (such as curriculum training and professional mentoring in the case of the ECE Cares initiative).

Use of Technology. Using Microsoft Excel, Access, or other spreadsheet software to create update forms, questionnaires, and surveys will make it easier to modify the format as needed. Consider sending written surveys via e-mail attachments, or put the survey right into the body of your message. If you and your survey respondents have the capacity, design a Web site that allows people to take surveys online—you'll save paper and time. The bottom line is, whatever tools and methods

6.7 Suggested Interview Questions for Focus Groups and Individuals

---

Suggested Interview Questions for Program *Personnel/Staff*

1. From your perspective, in what ways has the program been effective or successful? Please share specific examples.

2. In what ways has the program made progress toward the desired outcomes and indicators?

3. From your perspective, what challenges or concerns have you encountered with this program? Please describe.

4. What could be done to improve or enhance the program in the future?

5. Is there anything else that you would like to add at this time?

Suggested Interview Questions for Program *Participants*

1. What did you gain as a result of participation in this program/service/activity?

2. How do you anticipate using the knowledge/skills that you gained as a result of your participation in this program/service/activity? Please describe.

3. What aspect of this program/service/activity did you find to be most valuable? Least valuable?

4. What suggestions do you have for improving this program/service/activity in the future?

5. Would you recommend this program/service/activity to others? Please explain your response.

6. Is there anything else that you would like to add at this time?

---

you use to collect data, be sure they are easy to understand and are used consistently.

5. Collect and Analyze the Information About Project Achievements

It's essential to evaluate indicators early and throughout the implementation of your project. If you do not develop a data collection system during the grant application process or early in project implementation, it will be far more difficult to generate with accuracy the type of information you will need for intended users for intended purposes. If you establish from the beginning who will collect what types of evaluation data, how it will be collected, and the tools to use, there won't be a mad scramble to collect information and generate summaries when performance reports come due.

Use the tools described above, and any other quantitative and qualitative data collection strategies that you choose to employ, to collect the information about indicators of project achievement. As much as possible, organize and store the information in a central and electronically based location so that it will be easy to access and use. Once the information is collected, you must analyze (compile, reorganize, examine, and scrutinize) it to gauge the extent to which you are making progress toward short- and long-term project outcomes. The goal is to summarize what you have found as a result of analyzing the data.

Evaluation findings arc made up of the conclusions and observations about progress toward outcomes and the achievement of indicators that resulted from the analysis of the quantitative and qualitative data. Collecting and analyzing data can be very complex and time consuming. At this point, many projects, if they haven't already done so, seek the assistance of an external evaluator to analyze the data they have collected. In our experience, project personnel have the necessary skills to analyze their own information but usually don't make the time to fully exercise and dedicate those skills to project evaluation.

6. Disseminate and Utilize the Findings

The data that you gather and analyze about project indicators can be used to make decisions about program implementation and development; to judge the project's value, merit, and worth; or to inform the general debate around conceptual issues (such as increasing public awareness about the importance of quality early childhood education).

The evaluation findings will enable you to make informed midcourse adjustments in program implementation and help you to accurately showcase the effectiveness of your program's services and activities to funders.

But none of the inherent benefits of evaluation will be realized if the findings are not shared and used for some intended purpose. Whether your data are quantitative or qualitative, it is essential that you communicate evaluation findings to your primary intended users as soon as possible after the data are collected. It is quite likely that you will need to disseminate the information in a variety of ways. Funders may have annual or semi-annual performance reports with specific categories and boxes that you will need to fit your findings into. A board of directors or advisory group may want the evaluation findings in an executive summary format. You will also want to disseminate findings and share highlights through your media outlets—Web sites, newsletters, brochures, radio—so that a wider audience can learn about your project's achievements. Visit the Linking Learning to Life Web site (http://www. linkinglearningtolife.org) to see how the organization used evaluation findings to share and market project achievements. You can also use the evaluation findings at meetings of the project staff, management team, and executive committee to generate discussion about where the project is headed; to revisit outcomes, activities, and indicators; and to brainstorm how to improve programming. Whatever you do, don't sit on or file away the evaluation—share it and use it!

There's No Doubt About It— Evaluation Is Essential

Project personnel devote an incredible amount of time to the implementation of services and activities. They have a vested interest in knowing how things are going, whether the project is making a difference, and whether the participants have experienced success. Further, funders are increasingly expecting projects to rigorously assess and document their programmatic achievements. Yet when it comes to the essential activity of evaluation, many project directors do not know where to start.

For those brand new to the field of evaluation and assessment, consider visiting the online journal *Practical Assessment, Research and Evaluation* (http://pareonline.net/). It includes many helpful articles written in a user-friendly format on the topic of effective evaluation and assessment, including "Thinking About How to Evaluate Your Program? These Strategies Will Get You Started," by Rebecca Gajda (coauthor of this book) and Jennifer Jewiss (a seasoned health and human services evaluator and colleague of Rich and Rebecca's from the University of Vermont). You might also consider visiting the Web site of the American Evaluation Association at http://www.eval.org.

Key Points to Remember

❑ Every project needs to identify a qualified lead person who will be responsible for evaluation.

❑ It is essential to identify realistic project outcomes, key activities, and specific indicators to be evaluated.

❑ Evaluation has multiple purposes and can be used by many different people.

❑ Evaluation enables you to successfully (and relatively painlessly) respond to the funder's request for reporting data.

❑ Evaluation information can be used to strengthen the implementation and development of your project activities.

❑ Evaluation enhances the long-term sustainability of your initiative.

❑ Most important, effective evaluation increases the likelihood of achieving your desired outcomes and making a difference in the lives of those you serve.

7

Collaboration and Sustainability

> The ability to collaborate—on both a large and small scale—is one of the
> core requisites of post modern society. . . . In short, without collabora-
> tive skills and relationships it is not possible to learn and to continue to
> learn as much as you need in order to be an agent for social improvement.
> (Fullan, 1993, p. 17–18)

Maybe it seems obvious that collaboration is important and that partnerships cultivate long-term project success. So why have we written a whole
chapter on collaboration and sustainability?

We've learned from years of experience with grant applications, review,
and management that a "plan for sustainability" speaks to the creation of a
partnership-based project that engages all stakeholders and allows them to
make informed decisions about what to sustain and how to sustain it. Looking at sustainability as "where to find money once grant funds dry up" is a
limited and ineffective world view. Sustainability—the extent to which your
project and any or all of its elements can and will be maintained, continued,
carried on, nourished, and preserved—is directly related to the degree that
you have built genuine partnerships and collaboration with others.

Collaboration results in project ownership residing in multiple people
and organizations with a vested interest in a common vision. If partners
share your vision, they will make your needs their needs. If your partners
are invested in reaching shared project outcomes, they will find and share

human and physical resources, and publicize and market the project using their own organization's outlets. It is crucial that you cultivate shared investment and support for your project by building collaborative partnerships. This chapter will examine in great detail how to do this.

What Is Collaboration?

Collaboration can be a hard term to grasp; its definition is somewhat elusive, inconsistent, and theoretical. Generally overused, the term *collaboration* has become a catchall to signify just about any type of interorganizational or interpersonal relationship. This makes it difficult for those seeking to collaborate to know how to do it. Many people are not sure of what collaboration looks and feels like. They are not sure if their collective actions constitute true collaboration. For sustainability to become a reality, project leaders and stakeholders need to develop a common understanding of the characteristics of collaboration; only then will they be able to gauge the extent to which their partnerships are as healthy and productive as they could be.

Defining Collaboration

Collaboration signifies intentional interorganizational or interpersonal alliances created to benefit the partners and ultimately the stakeholders that they serve, but collaboration is known by many names. A brief look at a dictionary or a thesaurus reveals a whole host of definitions for the term *collaboration.* Its meaning is given as "working together," "a joint venture," "working jointly with others," "joining forces," "working in partnership," "pooling resources," "acting as a team," and "cooperating with one another."

Collaboration appears to signify just about any relationship between two entities, whether it is between two teachers who want new textbooks, three districts that seek to consolidate into one, or five high schools that want to make schools safer through combined after-school programming. And the terminology related to collaboration is extensive. These terms include *joint ventures, consolidations, networks, partnerships, coalitions, collaboratives, alliances, consortiums, associations, conglomerates, councils, task forces,* and *groups.* This list is not exhaustive, but it is exhausting to practitioners who seek to collaborate and who have the goal of increased collaboration written into their grant proposal and strategic plan. As such, project partners must come to a shared understanding of the nature of collaboration, be able to recognize its variations and complexities, and be able to put it to use as a vehicle for sustaining the initiative.

Collaboration Is About Communication Between People

It is people—not organizations—who collaborate. Without a basis for trust and healthy interpersonal connections between human beings, a strategic alliance is as effective as a two-legged stool. Trust is only developed between partners when there is time, effort, and energy put into the development of an accessible and functioning system for communication. As communication channels are developed and utilized, interpersonal conflict needs to be recognized as normal and even expected as the level of integration and personal involvement increases.

Chester Barnard, a former president of the New Jersey Bell Telephone Company and renowned organizational theorist, articulated three basic principles for effective communication in any initiative:

❑ Everyone should know what the channels of communication are.

❑ Everyone should have access to a formal channel of communication.

❑ Lines of communication should be as short and direct as possible. (One Pine, n.d.)

Everyone should know what the channels of communication are. A successful system of communication will have channels for staff, partners, and stakeholders to share ideas, information, and questions about project events and happenings, project successes, project development, and potential barriers to project success. Everyone should be clear about what type of information gets communicated, how it gets communicated, whom it gets communicated to, and when.

Everyone should have access to a formal channel of communication. The key terms here are *access*, which implies that every staff member, partner, and stakeholder has the opportunity to engage the channels of communication; and *formal,* which implies channels that are consistent and reliable. The initiative should provide the means and the opportunity for every staff member, partner, and stakeholder to express ideas, information, and questions.

Lines of communication should be as short and direct as possible. Whether formal or informal, all channels and means of organizational communication should be as straightforward and as nonbureaucratic as possible. Use the tools and media available at your school or in your district to streamline communication, including the following:

❑ Print (written or typed forms, letters, notes, newsletters, reports)

❑ Electronic (e-mail, Web sites, listservers)

❑ Voice (phone messaging, conference calling)

❑ Face-to-face (individual conferences, group meetings, informal "hallway" conversations)

Channels for communication need to be developed, articulated, accessed, and assessed regularly throughout the life of the initiative. Clear communication channels breed collaboration and sustainability. Effective channels for communication give people the means to have healthy relationships with one another.

Examples of Successful Collaborations

Looking at examples of successful small- and large-scale collaborations can help you understand the power of these kinds of relationships. Here we highlight two such examples.

College Connections

College Connections is one of the premier programs of Linking Learning to Life, a grant-funded, school-to-career nonprofit organization in Burlington, Vermont. The program enables high school students to take courses at area colleges while still in high school. Students earn college credit as well as credit toward high school graduation for successful course completion, and ongoing student supports are in place at both the high schools and the institutions of higher education. Most of the students enrolled in the program meet one or more target criteria: first-generation college attender, identified as having a disability, racial/ethnic minority, low-income family status, or ESL (English as a second language) learner.

The program idea was conceived six years ago with the collaborative input of high school students at risk of school failure, high school and college educators, the state financial aid agency, and area community-based organizations. The partnership sought and attained grant funding from a New England education foundation. College Connections has grown and evolved each year through the ongoing input of its advisory board members, representing multiple agencies and participating students. (Students provide input through a daily homeroom advisory, surveys about the program, and periodic focus forums to assess their experience and solicit recommendations.) The partnership members have worked closely together to secure funding from two major foundations and a state agency.

College Connections has expanded considerably since the first round of grant funding ended. The most significant actions taken that have led to its short- and long-term success include the following:

❑ Four partners (organizations other than Linking Leaning to Life) have initiated funding proposals to continue support for the program or included it in broader funding appeals.

❑ All six college/university partners have agreed to provide courses to participating students at substantially reduced tuition rates.

❑ Partner organizations have initiated several public relations and media pieces featuring the program.

❑ Participating high schools have changed policies to support awarding of academic credit for course completion.

❑ An area credit union joined the partnership to establish a matched college savings program for participating low-income students.

As a result of this collaborative effort, College Connections was selected as one of eight programs across the United States to be awarded planning and implementation grants and to participate in the Partnerships for College Access and Success initiative as an effective model. The project is funded by the Lumina Foundation for at least two years. The likelihood that College Connections will be sustained is greatly enhanced by the fact that it is "owned" and nurtured by many partners, not a single organization.

Safe Schools/Healthy Students Initiative

In 1999, just months after the episode of school violence at Columbine High School, the U.S. Departments of Education, Health and Human Services, and Justice launched an unprecedented joint endeavor called the Safe Schools/Healthy Students Initiative (SS/HSI). The SS/HSI demonstration grant initiative supports urban, rural, suburban, and tribal school district efforts to link prevention activities with integrated community-wide services and thus to strengthen local partnership approaches to violence prevention (Substance Abuse and Mental Health Services Administration [SAMHSA], 2004). On September 30, 2004, the U.S. Departments of Education, Health and Human Services, and Justice awarded an additional $38 million in grants to school districts

personnel who intend to offer comprehensive and coordinated services that involve partnerships among school districts, law enforcement agencies, and local mental health agencies (SAMHSA, 2004). The overarching goal of the nationwide Safe Schools/Healthy Students Initiative is to cultivate the effectiveness of collaborative community efforts in school violence prevention. Local SS/HS grant-funded projects such as the Larimer County Interagency Network for Kids (Project LINK) in Northern Colorado, funded in 1999 and Project PASS (Progress By Advancing Students and Schools) in Vermont funded in 2002, must demonstrate how community collaborative efforts develop, function, and bring about positive student and school level outcomes.

Collaboration and the Achievement of Outcomes

The types of issues that many school-based, grant-funded projects attempt to address may be confounded by dwindling local resources or high-pressure accountability mandates. To mitigate and address these issues requires team efforts. By working together, educators can pool scarce resources and minimize the duplication of services in order to achieve a vision and reach real outcomes that would not be possible to obtain if they worked separately. Whether your project involves 2 people or 20, there is no question that collaboration is the most effective way to address important societal issues and needs (Austin, 2000; Dufour & Eaker, 1998; Taylor-Powell, Rossing, & Geran, 1998).

The Stages of Collaboration

Whatever your project seeks to accomplish, it is likely that you and your partners will go through a process whereby you "form, storm, norm, and perform" together (Tuckman, 1965). It is important for project leaders to recognize that collaboration follows a natural and predictable pattern. You won't accomplish your activities or reach your outcomes overnight, so take the time to honor each stage of development. Project personnel are more likely to cultivate collaboration and long-term success when they recognize this developmental pattern as natural and expected. The stages of collaboration development have been more recently characterized as "assemble, order, perform, and transform" (Bailey & Koney, 2000).

Figure 7.1 summarizes the stages of collaboration through which successful educational partners can expect to progress.

In Stage 1, potential partners discuss the possibility of collaborating. Most grant applicants who have successfully responded to an RFP have found themselves in the throes of the assemble-and-form stage. In this stage, you and your potential partners ask yourselves questions about the value of coming together to take on a joint initiative, discuss the project's initial vision and mission, form an organizational structure, and begin to plan for the integration of resources. Once the initiative has successfully made it through the grant application process, it will naturally move into Stage 2 of collaboration development.

Stage 2 can be characterized as interpersonally and interorganizationally intense. This is when lots of activity and rapid change (or "storming") will take place. Each staff member, partner, and stakeholder maneuvers

7.1 Stages of Collaboration Development

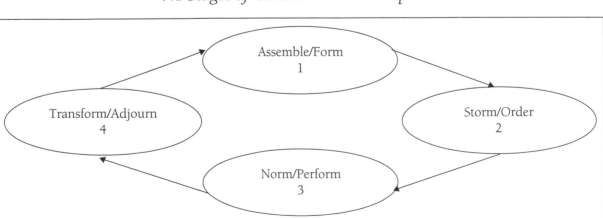

personally and professionally to establish a vital and viable role in the project. Formal memoranda of understanding need to be crafted, and the outcomes, activities, and indicators of the collaborative effort are developed and documented. Stage 2 is usually when projects go through the process of hiring personnel, securing physical space, and pooling partner resources.

In Stage 3, project partners and staff establish working norms and focus their energy on launching project activities and services. It is in this phase that the initiative begins the ongoing process of project implementation and renewal, which includes dialogue, decision making, action, and evaluation. Program evaluation is an essential element of this stage of collaborative development. And it is in this stage that communication channels are developed, articulated, accessed, and assessed.

In Stage 4 of collaboration development, project stakeholders work with evaluation and assessment findings and data to formally reassess and determine how to effectively transform the activities, strategies, and structures of the project. In this phase, project partners revisit the strategic plan to decide how best to support the continuation of the initiative, and they make decisions about what services and activities to maintain, expand, or discontinue. Sometimes it is perfectly appropriate to discontinue or end a project. Grant funds may have been provided for a discrete activity or purchase that does not need continuation. As

a teacher, Rebecca was the recipient of local grants intended to provide a team of teachers across a school district with seed money to improve pre-existing curricular materials for a dropout prevention program. When the partners determined that their needs had been met and project outcomes had been obtained (an inclusive curriculum was piloted that demonstrated increased student achievement), they decided to discontinue the collaborative effort.

It is important to keep in mind that all groups will pass through predictable stages before they can claim true collaboration. Successful engagement in each of these phases increases the likelihood of true and sustainable collaboration.

Assessing Collaboration

As the most effective classroom teachers tell us, assessment of student learning is the backbone of effective instruction. What good is cooperative learning, group discussion, an engaging lecture, or any other activity if we can't tell what students know and how they've come to know it as a result of our instruction? And so it goes with collaboration. Collaboration is only as healthy as we determine it to be through ongoing authentic assessment.

You can build a plan for assessing collaboration over time into your overall plan for evaluation (see Chapter 6). You may want to follow a process that is being used to assess collaboration in the SS/HSI, 21st Century

Community Learning Centers, the Centers for Disease Control and Prevention Research Centers, and other initiatives that capitalize on the power of collaboration. The heart of this process is the Collaboration Assessment Rubric, shown in Figure 7.2. You can use this assessment tool to evaluate collaboration in each stage of partnership development, as part of your comprehensive evaluation plan.

A Process for Evaluating Collaboration

Shortly after an alliance forms and has entered the ordering phase, you can bring representatives from all of the project's key agencies and entities together for professional development focused on collaboration. Using the Collaboration Assessment Rubric as a guide, participants discuss and assess their current level of integration and speculate on their desired level of integration in the future. Participants' perceptions of the current and the desired levels of integration between their agency and all the other partners are compiled and recorded.

During the norming/performing and transforming/adjourning stages of alliance development, you periodically can repeat this process of assessing collaboration (both quantitatively and qualitatively) over time. Partners (old and new) will become reacquainted with existing team members, and all the partners will come to better understand the overarching goals of the initiative and the growth made thus far. Additionally, all members of the alliance will benefit from a review of the multiple meanings of collaboration and a chance to identify and describe examples of collaborative success and change. In subsequent assessment of collaboration, post-baseline data for the initiative can be identified and recorded, which allows project staff and partners to ascertain and celebrate the growth in their collaborative efforts over time.

This process of assessing levels of integration requires a substantial amount of time and space for project partners to meet and engage in thoughtful and thorough discussion with one another. If you are working with a program evaluator, the evaluator can use the Collaboration Assessment Rubric to encourage partners to express their perceptions of levels of collaboration, to collect comprehensive baseline data about collaboration, and to clear up projectwide misconceptions and confusion about the meaning of collaboration.

A Safe Schools/Healthy Students Example

The project partners who received funds through the Safe Schools/Healthy Students local initiatives that were described earlier in this chapter are collaborating in their efforts to create safe and healthy school conditions for children. Over the course of the grant funding period, they expect to see evidence of increased collaboration and have articulated this as an outcome in their respective evaluation plans. These SS/HSI partners recognize

7.2 Collaboration Assessment Rubric

Level of Collaboration	Purpose	Strategies and Tasks	Leadership and Decision Making	Interpersonal and Communication
Networking 1	Create a web of communication Identify and create a base of support Explore interests	Loose or no structure Flexible; undefined roles Few if any defined tasks	Nonhierarchical Flexible Minimal or no group decision making	Very little interpersonal conflict Communication among all members infrequent or absent
Cooperating 2	Work together to ensure tasks are done Leverage or raise money Identify mutual needs, but maintain separate identities	Advisory member links Minimal structure Some strategies and tasks identified	Nonhierarchical; decisions generally low stakes Facilitative leaders, usually volunteers "Go-to" hub formed by several people	Some degree of personal commitment and investment Minimal interpersonal conflict Communication among members clear, but may be informal
Partnering 3	Share resources to address common issues Remain autonomous but support something new Reach mutual goals together	Strategies and tasks developed and maintained Central body of people Central body of people with specific tasks	Autonomous leadership Alliance members sharing equally in decision making Decision-making mechanisms in place	Some interpersonal conflict Communication system and formal information channels developed Evidence of problem solving and productivity
Merging 4	Merge resources to create or support something new Extract money from existing systems/ members Commit for a long period of time to achieve short- and long-term outcomes	Formal structure to support strategies and tasks Specific and complex strategies and tasks identified Committees and subcommittees formed	Strong, visible leadership Sharing and delegation of roles and responsibilities Leadership that capitalizes upon diversity and organizational strengths	High degree of commitment and investment Possibility of interpersonal conflict high Communication that is clear, frequent, and prioritized High degree of problem solving and productivity
Unifying 5	Unite or acquire to form a single structure Relinquish autonomy to support surviving organization	Highly formal, legally complex Permanent reorganization of strategies and tasks	Central, typically hierarchical leadership Leadership that capitalizes upon diversity and organizational strengths	Possibility of interpersonal conflict very high Communication that is clear, frequent, prioritized, formal, and informal

Source: R. Gajda, Utilizing collaboration theory to evaluate strategic alliances, American Journal of Evaluation 25(1), p. 71, © 2004. Adapted with permission from the publisher.

collaboration as both the vehicle for obtaining student and school-level outcomes and a long-term outcome itself. And the federal funding agencies require that they evaluate collaboration toward these ends.

Larimer County Interagency Network for Kids (Project LINK), a Safe Schools/Healthy Students initiative in Colorado, integrated the use of the Collaboration Assessment Rubric throughout project implementation in order to assess the strength of its school-community collaboration over time. Project LINK partners include the Poudre School District, the Larimer County Sheriff's Department, the Fort Collins Police Department, Visiting Nurse Association, Colorado State University, and community mental health agencies. Throughout the forming, storming, norming, performing, and transforming stages of Project LINK development (see Figure 7.1), an interagency group of key representatives consistently met to renew their collective understanding of collaboration and discuss perceptions about the purpose, strategies/tasks, leadership/decision-making, and interpersonal dynamics/communication of their safe schools alliance.

The interagency group that gathers at the semi-annual "collaboration assessment meetings" uses the Collaboration Assessment Rubric to collect qualitative and quantitative data about their collaborative efforts. To collect the data, Project LINK partners work together to numerically assess on a scale of 1–5 their *current* level of interorganizational integration and to discuss their *desired* or ideal level of integration. Group members attempt to reach consensus on the current level of integration and desired long term level of integration between their agencies and organizations. After current and desired levels of integration are numerically recorded, strategic alliance partners engage in discussion and then document in writing the structural and procedural steps they anticipate needing to take in order to move toward their ideal level of integration. To prompt discussion on this task, partners ask themselves: *What would it look like if we reached our ideal level of collaboration? What actions do we need and want to take to bring about our ideal desired level of collaboration? What is the evidence that would indicate to us that we have reached our ideal level of collaboration?* Group members spend a concerted amount of time in thoughtful discussion conferring about how to build greater levels of collaboration between project partners.

The data generated by this ongoing process of collaboration assessment gives partners the opportunity to see where and how growth in collaboration occurs. In Project LINK, educational partners discovered and documented that over the course of the first year of implementation, the overall composite level of Project LINK collaboration grew from networking (1) to cooperating (2). The level of collaboration rose to partnering (3) by the end of the second year of formal partnerships between school district, law enforcement, and other community partners (Research and Development Center, 2002). Through collaboration assessment, partnering agencies have come to realize that universally high levels of collaboration might not be necessary to reduce youth violence or achieve other identified outcomes. In Project LINK, partners learned that although it sounded politically correct to form a "collaborative," their goals could be achieved with well developed cooperation (level 2) or partnering (level 3). For example, the School Resources Officers found that a "network" was a sufficient level of integration to have with the Nurse Home Visitation liaisons. This realization meant that financial resources that would have been targeted for building the structure (e.g., listserv, Web site, or sub-committee development) to support higher levels of integration could be used for direct services such as hiring an additional School Resource Officer.

KEY POINTS TO REMEMBER

❑ Collaboration is an imperative and leads to realization of project outcomes.

❑ Community needs are more likely to be successfully addressed through collaborative efforts.

❑ Collaboration is predicated on healthy interpersonal relationships and an effective system for communication.

❑ Collaboration develops in natural stages.

❑ Assessing collaboration over time cultivates collaboration over time.

❑ Most funders consider collaboration crucial to project success and incorporate it into their RFP and grant application packages.

Glossary

Activities. Services that your project delivers and provides to reach short- and long-term participant outcomes.

Allowable costs. Types of expenses that you can pay for with grant funds. Many grant requests also specify "not allowable" costs, which you cannot pay for with grant funds.

Applicant. The person, organization, or partnership that is submitting a grant application for funding.

Appropriation. The amount of funds that are authorized to be spent by Congress, in the case of federal grants; by the state legislature, in the case of state grants; or by municipal authorities, in the case of local government grants.

Assurances. Set statements that you as the grant applicant must sign, especially for federal and state grants, that assure that you will abide by laws pertaining to the use of these funds. Some examples are statements associated with Drug-Free Workplace, Title IX, lobbying, and nondiscrimination.

CFDA number. An assigned number associated with each grant in the Catalog of Federal Domestic Assistance, a listing published by the federal government of all grants available through all federal agencies and departments.

Collaboration. A process by which partners come together to deliver services and undertake activities to reach shared outcomes that would not be possible if they worked separately. Sometimes referred to as "strategic alliance."

Community Foundation. An organization that is created to fund projects in the local area that address community needs.

Concept paper. An initial description of a project idea that at least outlines the what, why, and for whom of the project.

Contract. A written agreement that requires specified tasks to be accomplished or levels of performance to be reached by certain time lines for the person or organization issuing the contract.

Demonstration grant. A category of federal grants that are designed to support new projects or ideas as potential good examples for others to replicate.

Direct costs. Expenses needed to carry out the core work of the project.

These include items such as salary and fringe benefits for staff, supplies, project-related travel, equipment, curriculum materials, copying, printing, postage, and meeting costs. (See also **indirect costs.**)

Dissemination. Sharing the results or products of your work; getting the word out to a broader audience about what you have accomplished. Some grantors will ask you to identify up front to whom you will disseminate your results. This term is also used to define a category of federal grants.

EDGAR (Education Department General Administrative Regulations). Regulations that govern U.S. Department of Education programs and the grants associated with these programs.

Evaluation plan. The development of a systematic process of assessment whereby information about project outcomes, activities, and indicators is collected, analyzed, and reported. The process of evaluation planning, data collection, data analysis, and dissemination should be carried out intentionally. (See Chapter 6.)

Federal Register. A daily newspaper produced by the federal government. It details the latest rules and regulations related to grants through all federal government agencies, invitations for public comment, and the actual RFPs for grants to be awarded. It is available online at http://www.gpoaccess.gov/nara/index.html.

Funder. The organization, agency, or individual providing money to others to carry out their projects. It is used interchangeably with **grantor**. There are federal, state, local, corporate, and private foundation funders.

Grant. An award, usually in the form of money, that comes with the assurance that it will be used according to specific guidelines that are agreed to up front. Most grants are awarded in response to an RFP. (See also **RFP.**)

Grantor. An organization, agency, or individual that is providing awards of money or other resources to those requesting it. There are many different kinds of grantors, both public and private. The term is used interchangeably with **funder**.

Indicators. The gauge as to whether, to what degree, and in what ways your project is carrying out its activities and making progress toward its outcomes. Indicators can be both quantitative and qualitative; therefore, they can be represented by both statistics and narratives.

Indirect costs. Costs that are not directly related to running the project but are necessary to be able to host and manage it. Examples include items such as a portion of the rent, electricity, and maintenance for the space occupied; accounting, reporting, and audit costs related to managing grant funds; or a portion of the organization's insurance expenses. Some grant requests do not allow for the inclusion of indirect costs in your budget. Others will specify that indirect costs not exceed a specific percentage of direct costs. (See also **direct costs.**)

In-kind or matching contributions. Funds or other resources that the grant applicant is contributing to partially support the project. Many grantors will require some amount of matching contributions, and it may be very specific in dollar amount or percentage of funds requested.

Labor market. A designated area of local economic activity defined by the state or federal government.

Lead evaluator. The person responsible for the development and enactment of the evaluation plan. This person can be from inside or outside of the organization.

Memorandum of understanding (MOU) or letter of agreement (LOA). A signed agreement among two or more partners that delineates the roles and responsibilities of each. (See Chapter 5.)

Organizational structure. The configuration and composition of project management that provides the capacity for effective management, budgeting, marketing, strategic planning, and evaluation. As the scope and scale of a project increase, so should the complexity of the organizational structure. (See Chapter 5.)

Outcomes. The intended, clearly defined, anticipated, and desired impacts of the project on participants. Outcomes focus on the realization of measurable and observable participant benefits.

Peer review. The process by which most grant proposals are reviewed within the federal government structure. This structure is sometimes used for state grants and other types as well. (See Chapter 4.)

Performance report. Required documentation provided to funders, usually annually or semiannually, that describes the project's accomplishments and documents performance.

Philanthropists. Individuals who commit personal resources for the common good.

Pilot project. A new program or project that is being created to test its value or effectiveness. If successful, the intent is usually to maintain or expand the pilot.

Principal investigator. The person who is assigned direct control over a project or a portion of a project. This term is most frequently used in certain types of federal grants.

Proposal. The application for funding that is submitted with the hope of receiving a grant. The proposal represents a direct response to the items detailed in a Request for Proposals, or RFP. (See also **RFP**.)

Public domain. Information that literally "belongs to the public." A great deal of information that is generated by local, state, and federal government entities, including school districts, is in the public domain and can therefore be directly accessed or requested from these government entities.

Qualitative data. Evaluation-related information about project outcomes, activities, and indicators, presented in the form of words and narrative.

Quantitative data. Evaluation-related information about project outcomes, activities, and indicators, presented in the form of numbers and statistics.

Replication. The process of implementing in your own setting a model project from another school or community.

RFP (Request for Proposals). The invitation by a grantor to submit an application or proposal to receive funding. The RFP provides the guidelines for all of the information you need to include in your proposal in order to be considered for funding. It also specifies deadlines for submitting your proposal and delivery instructions and may include formatting specifications for writing your proposal (e.g., size of margins, spacing, size of font), attachments required (e.g., letters of support, staff résumés, promotional materials, fiscal reports), and other essential information. (See Chapter 3.)

Seed grants/money. Funds specifically designated to get a project started. Seed grants may be provided for as long as three to five years, depending on the nature of the project, but more typically are for the first year or two to get a project up and running.

Selection criteria. The standards that reviewers must use to evaluate the quality of your proposal. Often point values are attached to each of the selection criteria components (e.g., Statement of Purpose—10 points, Project Design—25 points, Management Plan—20 points). (See Chapters 3 and 4.)

Stakeholders. Those individuals and organizations who have a vested interest in the project and who are affected (directly and indirectly) by its operations.

Sustainability. The cultivation of shared investment and project support through the formation of collaborative partnerships. (See Chapter 7.)

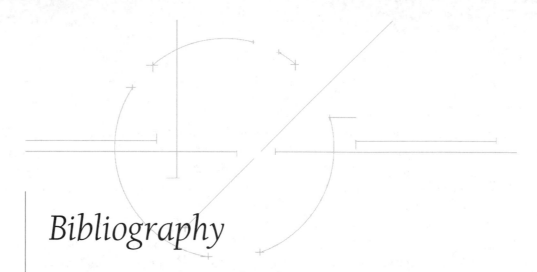

Bibliography

Allen, R. (2003, March). Funding innovation. *Education Update 45*(2), 1, 3, 8.

Austin, J. (2000). *The collaboration challenge: How non-profits and businesses succeed through strategic alliances.* San Francisco: Jossey-Bass.

Bailey, D., & Koney, K. (2000). *Strategic alliances among health and human services organizations: From affiliations to consolidations* [Abridged]. Thousand Oaks, CA: Sage Publications.

Calabrese, R. (2000). *Leadership for safe schools: A community-based approach.* Lanham, MD: Scarecrow Press.

CD Publications (2003). Children and Youth Funding Report. Silver Spring, MD: Author.

Chalker, D. (1999). *Leadership for rural schools: Lessons for all educators.* Lanham, MD: Scarecrow Press.

Dryfoos, J. (1998). *Safe passage: Making it through adolescence in a risky society.* New York: Oxford University Press.

Dufour, R., & Eaker, R. (1998). *Professional Learning Communities at Work: Best Practices for Enhancing Student Achievement.* Bloomington, IN: National Education Service; Alexandria, VA: ASCD.

Foundation Center. (2003). *Annual Report.* Retrieved July 15, 2004, from http://fdncenter.org/about/FCAR03.pdf.

Fullan, M. (1993). *Change forces: Probing the depths of educational reform.* New York: Routledge Falmer.

Gajda, R. (2004, Spring). Utilizing collaboration theory to evaluate strategic alliances. *American Journal of Evaluation 25*(1), 65–77.

Gajda, R., & Jewiss, J. (2004). Thinking about how to evaluate your program? These strategies will get you started. *Practical Assessment, Research &Evaluation 9*(8). Available online at http://pareonline.net/getvn.asp?v=9&n=8.

Grant makers reveal the most common reasons grant proposals get rejected. (2003). *The Chronicle of Philanthropy.* Retrieved May 1, 2003, from http://philanthropy.com/jobs/2003/05/01/20030523-378096.htm.

Hall, M. (1988). *Getting funded: A complete guide to proposal writing.* Portland, OR: Portland State University, Continuing Education Publications.

Harper's Index. (2004, August). *Harper's Magazine, 3*.

Hesselbein, F., & Whitehead, J. (2000). Foreword. In James Austin, *The collaboration challenge: How non-profits and businesses succeed through strategic alliances.* San Francisco: Jossey-Bass.

Hogue, T., Perkins, D., Clark, R., Bergstrum, A., Slinkski, M., & Associates. (1995). *Collaboration framework: Addressing community capacity.* Columbus, OH: National Network for Collaboration.

One Pine (n.d.). Retrieved February 17, 2005, from http://www.onepine.info/pbarnard.htm.

Orlich, D. (2002). *Designing successful grant proposals.* Alexandria, VA: Association for Supervision and Curriculum Development.

Patton, M. (1997). *Utilization-focused evaluation: The new century text* (3rd ed.). Thousand Oaks, CA: Sage Publications.

Research and Development Center. (2002). *Project LINK Safe Schools/Healthy Students: Year two evaluation report.* Retrieved February 26, 2003, from http://www.colostate.edu/depts/r-dcenter/LINKFinal%20ReportYR2.pdf.

Research Triangle Institute. (2003). *Safe Schools/Healthy Students Initiative.* Retrieved February 1, 2003, from http://www.sshsevaluation.org.

Substance Abuse and Mental Health Services Administration [SAMHSA]. (2004). Retrieved May 20, 2005, from http://www.sshs.samhsa.gov.

Taylor-Powell, E., Rossing, B., & Geran, J. (1998). *Evaluating collaboratives: Reaching the potential.* Madison, WI: Program Development and Evaluation, University of Wisconsin Extension.

Tuckman, B. (1965). Developmental sequence in small groups. *Psychological Bulletin 63*(6), 384–399.

Weiss, H. B. (2004, Spring). From the director's desk. *The Evaluation Exchange 10*(1). Harvard Family Research Project. Harvard Graduate School of Education.

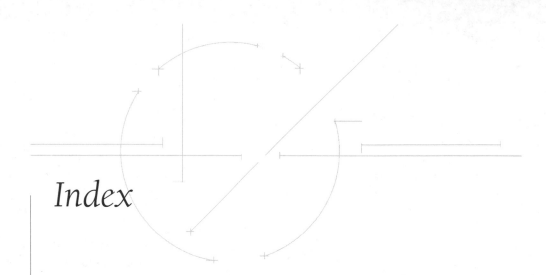

Index

Note: An *f* following a page number indicates a figure.

About the Authors

Rebecca Gajda is an Assistant Professor in the Secondary Education and Educational Leadership Programs in the College of Education and Social Services at the University of Vermont. She teaches graduate and undergraduate courses in curriculum, instruction, and assessment. She has a master's degree in special education and spent many years developing and teaching in programs for children at risk. She was the Education Codirector at Youth S.A.F.E., a shelter for homeless and abused children and adolescents, and the dropout prevention coordinator for a large, demographically diverse school district in Colorado for several years.

Rebecca earned her Ph.D. in Educational Leadership at Colorado State University, where she specialized in teacher education and staff development. While earning her degree she was the Senior Research Associate at the Research and Development Center for the Advancement of Student Learning, where she directed local, state, and national grant-sponsored evaluation projects. She has been responsible for the management and/or evaluation of multimillion-dollar federally sponsored initiatives, including the Safe Schools/Healthy Students (SS/HS) and 21st Century Community Learning Centers (21st CCLC) demonstration grants. She has been a technical grant writer and lead evaluator for a wide range of public and privately funded educational and school renewal initiatives that have tackled such issues as teacher mentoring, school-to-work, career academies, and preK–16 educational partnerships. In addition, she has been a federal grant reviewer for several national grant competitions sponsored by the U.S. Department of Education. Rebecca is a former secondary social studies teacher and received her first grant during her second year of teaching; it provided her with $500 to buy 15 books, two posters, and miscellaneous supplies for her alternative education class for 9th graders at risk of dropping out.

Rebecca's current educational work involves program evaluation, high school renewal, professional development, and curricular leadership in the schools. In addition, she focuses much of her time on developing, leading, and sustaining grant-sponsored initiatives that work in the interest of children, families, and teachers. She is an active member of the Association for Supervision and Curriculum Development, the American Evaluation Association, and the American Association of Colleges for Teacher Education. Rebecca can be reached at Rebecca.Gajda@uvm.edu or by phone at 802-656-1424.

Richard Tulikangas is the current and founding Executive Director of Linking Learning to Life, Inc., a nonprofit organization whose mission is to improve the educational and employment outcomes for K–12 students in the Lake Champlain region of Vermont. The organization develops, coordinates, and manages a wide range of applied learning, career development, and community-based learning programs and services for youth. Some of these are specifically designed for young people who face various challenges and barriers to educational and employment success. In addition to the other responsibilities of running a nonprofit, Rich is constantly identifying, pursuing, and securing resources needed to sustain the organization. In this role he has secured funding from more than 25 different sources, public and private, corporate and governmental. Successful grant writing has secured the vast majority of funding for Linking Learning to Life. Rich earned an M.Ed. in organizational and human resources development from the University of Vermont and a B.S. in natural resources from the University of Michigan.

Previously Rich worked for 10 years in the Vermont Department of Education and was responsible at various times for cooperative vocational education, youth employment programs, and school restructuring and improvement initiatives. He led the Reinventing Vermont Schools Initiative, a statewide effort to help schools transform education locally in order to improve student outcomes. Rich was responsible for creating statewide programs that gave high school students new opportunities to connect their academic experience to real-life applications in their own communities.

Rich also managed grant-funded youth programs for the Vermont Department of Education, and in this capacity reviewed, responded to, and advised schools and community organizations across the state as subgrantees. Beginning in 1995 he was "on loan" to the Vermont Governor's Office for 18 months to build a statewide school-to-work partnership among six state agencies and numerous regional groups, businesses, and school districts. This in turn led to developing and submitting a successful five-year, multimillion-dollar National School-to-Work Opportunities Act grant that helps prepare all students for life beyond high school. Rich had the good fortune, in a sense, of managing grant-funded programs before ever having to write a grant of his own. He managed statewide youth employment and career development programs that subgranted funds to local schools and community organizations across the state. Rich can be reached at rtulikan@bsdvt.org or by phone at 802-951-8850.

Related ASCD Resources: Grants

At the time of publication, the following ASCD resources were available; for the most up-to-date information about ASCD resources, go to www.ascd.org. ASCD stock numbers are noted in parentheses.

Audio

Funding Innovation: Grant Writing in the Information Age Sheryl Abshire (Audiotape #204185, CD #504319)

Networks

Visit the ASCD Web site (www.ascd.org) and click on About ASCD. Under the header of Your Partnership with ASCD, click on Networks for information about professional educators who have formed groups around topics, including "Invitational Education." Look in the "Network Directory" for current facilitators' addresses and phone numbers.

Print Products

Designing Successful Grant Proposals Donald C. Orlich (#196022)
Education Update March 2003 Funding Innovation (#103041)

For additional resources, visit us on the World Wide Web (http://www.ascd.org), send an e-mail message to member@ascd.org, call the ASCD Service Center (1-800-933-ASCD or 703-578-9600, then press 2), send a fax to 703-575-5400, or write to Information Services, ASCD, 1703 N. Beauregard St., Alexandria, VA 22311-1714 USA.